W9-BKZ-283

The Essential WW Freestyle™ Cookbook

150 Dishes in 30 Minutes or Less Using Zero Points® Foods

WW Publishing Group

Edit

VP Content/Editor in Chief **Theresa DiMasi**

Managing Editor **Valeria Bloom**

Food Editor **Eileen Runyan**

Writer and Project Editor **Jackie Mills, MS, RD**

Contributing Editors **Lisa Chernick, Leslie Fink, MS, RD**

Assistant Editor **Nathan Zucker**

Contributing Writer **Colin Spagnoli**

Nutrition Consultant **Laureen Jean Leyden**

Recipe Developers **Dina Cheney, Angela Nilsen, Carol Prager, Julia Rutland**

Art

Creative Director, Content **Denis Darch**

Creative Director **Ed Melnitsky**

Design Director **Daniela A. Hritcu**

Designer **Rebecca Kollmer**

Production Manager **Alan Biederman**

Photo

Photo/On-set Art Director **Marybeth Dulany**

Photographer **Christopher Testani**

Food Stylist **Chris Lanier**

Prop Stylist **Philippa Brathwaite**

© Copyright 2018 Weight Watchers International, Inc.

Nothing may be reprinted in whole or in part without permission from the publisher. Editorial and art produced by W/W Twentyfirst Corp., 675 Avenue of the Americas, New York, NY 10010.

The WW Coin Logo, WW Freestyle, and SmartPoints trademarks are the registered trademarks of Weight Watchers International, Inc.

SKU #9061000

Printed in the USA

Front cover:
Chicken with strawberry-balsamic salsa, page 4

Back cover:
Edamame and couscous salad with feta, page 122

Tomato and
ricotta frittata,
page 151

About WW

Weight Watchers is a global wellness company and the world's leading commercial weight management program. We inspire millions of people to adopt healthy habits for real life. Through our engaging digital experience and face-to-face group meetings, members follow our livable and sustainable program that encompasses healthy eating, physical activity and positive mindset. With more than five decades of experience in building communities and our deep expertise in behavioral science, we aim to deliver wellness for all. To learn more about the Weight Watchers approach to healthy living, please visit www.weightwatchers.com. For more information about our global business, visit our corporate website at www.weightwatchersinternational.com.

Blueberries with ricotta
and balsamic glaze,
page 249

Contents

A new way to cook & eat

Eating delicious food is one of life's greatest pleasures. In a perfect world, healthy and tasty food would surround us and it would be easy to know what to eat.

Unfortunately, that's not always the case. Too often we worry about what we're eating—is it nutritious, is it organic, is it undercooked, is it overcooked, is it safe, can we afford it, can we find fresh fruits and vegetables? We label a food healthy or unhealthy and tell ourselves we should eat this, and we shouldn't eat that, and if we do end up eating a "bad" food, we feel badly about it, especially if we're trying to lose weight and lead a healthier lifestyle. There are hundreds of reasons that keep us from enjoying the foods we love.

That's where Weight Watchers can help: We think our new WW Freestyle program which is designed around healthy choices, and this companion cookbook will make deciding what to eat (and what to cook) much easier. By giving you recipes that work with the new program, we hope to relieve any anxiety you might have when your family asks, "What's for dinner?" Sure, sometimes you want to cook purely for the pleasure of it, but often you just want to make something simple, satisfying, and in line with your SmartPoints® Budget. Now you can do both. We believe you can eat delicious food and feel good about it, and that the choices you make ought to be between which favorite food to eat, not between pleasure or deprivation.

We've organized this book into chapters that feature foods with a SmartPoints value of 0: skinless chicken and turkey, seafood, plant-based proteins, eggs, veggies, unsweetened fat-free plain yogurt, and fruits. These go-to foods do not need to be tracked or measured—you can work them into your menu as often as you like, and track only the foods with SmartPoints values that you use to accompany these ingredients. We also give you key tools and techniques for making the most out of these zero Points foods. In these pages, you'll learn:

- The secret to moist chicken breast
- How make flaky, flavor-filled fish
- The best way to avoid squishy tofu
- How to make the perfect omelette
- Ten favorite stir-ins for unsweetened plain fat-free yogurt
- How to add veggies to almost anything
- How to shop for, store, and enjoy fruit at its peak flavor

Each dish emphasizes what we value most at Weight Watchers—health, freshness, quality, and maximum flavor—while being unfussy, easy to shop for, and ready in under 30 minutes. Many recipes include notes on ingredients, make-ahead strategies, or shortcuts. Use them as inspiration for your own creations. Our hope is that this cookbook helps you think differently about cooking, and encourages you to approach the kitchen with confidence, humor, and a sense of adventure.

For me, a good home-cooked meal nourishes me physically and emotionally, and eating the foods I love gives me a sense of abundance and freedom. Find what works for you and, hopefully, you'll feel that freedom, too.

Enjoy!

Theresa DiMasi
EDITOR IN CHIEF/VP CONTENT

Spanikopita
quesadillas,
page 177

About our recipes

While losing weight isn't only about what you eat, Weight Watchers realizes the critical role it plays in your success and overall good health. That's why our philosophy is to offer great-tasting, easy recipes that are nutritious as well as delicious. Our recipes emphasize the kinds of healthy ingredients we love: lots of fresh fruits and vegetables, most of which are zero Points foods, and lean proteins, some of which have 0 SmartPoints and others that are low in SmartPoints. We also try to ensure that our recipes fall within the recommendations of the U.S. Dietary Guidelines for Americans—lower in saturated fat and sugar with plenty of fruits and vegetables, lean proteins, and low-fat dairy—so they support a diet that promotes health and reduces the risk for disease. If you have special dietary needs, consult with your health-care professional for advice on a diet that is best for you, then adapt these recipes to meet your specific nutritional needs.

Get started, keep going, and enjoy good nutrition

At Weight Watchers, we believe that eating well makes life better, no matter where you are in your weight-loss journey. These tasty recipes are ideal, whether you're just getting started or have already reached your goals on the SmartPoints system. Unlike other weight-loss programs, which focus solely on calories, the SmartPoints system guides you toward healthier foods that are lower in sugar and saturated fat, and higher in protein. But this isn't a diet—all food is "in." Eating well should be fun, energizing, and delicious, so that healthy food choices become second nature. To get maximum satisfaction, we suggest you keep the following information in mind while preparing our recipes:

- On the WW Freestyle™ program, eating a mix of foods (rather than all zero Points meals) can help you avoid feeling bored or deprived. Remember, there's room for all SmartPoints foods in your plan—variety is key to a healthy and livable eating style.

- SmartPoints values are given for each recipe. The SmartPoints value for each ingredient is assigned based on the number of calories and the amount of saturated fat, sugar, and protein in each ingredient. The SmartPoints value for each ingredient is then added together and divided by the number of servings, and the result is rounded.

- Recipes include approximate nutritional information: They are analyzed for Calories (Cal), Total Fat, Saturated Fat (Sat Fat), Sodium (Sod), Total Carbohydrates (Total Carb), Sugar, Dietary Fiber (Fib), and Protein (Prot). The nutritional values are obtained from the Weight Watchers database, which is maintained by registered dietitians.

- To boost flavor, we often include fresh herbs or a squeeze of citrus instead of increasing the salt. If you don't need to restrict your sodium intake, feel free to add a touch more salt as desired.

- Recipes in this book that are designated gluten free do not contain any wheat (in all forms, including kamut, semolina, spelt, and triticale), barley, or rye, or any products that are made from these ingredients, such as breads, couscous, pastas, seitan, soy sauce, beer, malt vinegar, and malt beverages. Other foods such as salad dressings, Asian-style sauces, salsa and tomato sauce, shredded cheese, yogurt, and sour cream may be sources of gluten. Check ingredient labels carefully on packaged foods that we call for, as different brands of the same premade food product may or may not contain gluten. If you are following a gluten-free diet because you have celiac disease, please consult your health-care professional.

- Recipe introductory headnote suggestions and Freestyle It tips have a SmartPoints value of 0 unless otherwise stated.

- For information about the Weight Watchers plan, please visit WeightWatchers.com/us/m/cms/plan-basics.

Calculations not what you expected?

SmartPoints value for the recipes in this book are calculated without counting the zero Points foods—fruits, most vegetables, and some lean proteins that are part of the plan. However, the nutritional information does include the nutrient content of these ingredients. This means you may notice discrepancies with the SmartPoints value you calculate using the nutrition information provided for the recipe versus the SmartPoints value listed for the recipe. That's because the SmartPoints value for the recipes that contain zero Points ingredients have been adjusted to reflect those ingredients, while the nutrition information provided includes the nutrition for all of the ingredients. For tracking purposes, use the SmartPoints value listed for the recipe. Also, please note, when fruits and veggies are liquefied or pureed (as in a smoothie), their nutrient content is incorporated into the recipe calculations. These nutrients can increase the SmartPoints value.

Alcohol is included in our SmartPoints value calculations. Because alcohol information is generally not included on nutrition labels, it's not an option you can include when using the handheld or online SmartPoints calculator or the Weight Watchers app. But since we include the alcohol information that we get from our database in our recipes, you might notice discrepancies between the SmartPoints value you see here in our recipes and the value you get using the calculator. The SmartPoints listed for our recipes are the most accurate.

Simply Filling (the no-count option)

If counting SmartPoints isn't your thing, try Simply Filling, a no-count technique. To follow it, eat just until satisfied, primarily from the list of Simply Filling foods found in the Tracker online. For more information, see your meeting-room materials or go online if you are a subscriber.

Choosing ingredients

As you learn to eat more healthfully and add more wholesome foods to your meals, consider these:

- **Lean meats and poultry**
  Purchase lean meats and poultry, and trim them of all visible fat before cooking. When poultry is cooked with the skin on, we recommend removing the skin before eating. Nutritional information for recipes that include meat, poultry, and fish is based on cooked skinless, boneless portions (unless otherwise stated) with the fat trimmed.

- **Seafood**
  Whenever possible, our recipes call for seafood that is sustainable and deemed the most healthful for human consumption so that your choice of seafood is not only good for the oceans but also good for you. For more information about the best seafood choices and to download a pocket guide, go to the Environmental Defense Fund at seafood.edf.org, the Monterey Bay Aquarium at seafoodwatch.org, or the Safina Center at safinacenter.org.

- **Produce**
  For the best flavor, maximum nutrient content, and the lowest prices, buy fresh, local produce such as vegetables, leafy greens, and fruits in season. Rinse them thoroughly before using, and keep a supply of cut-up vegetables and fruits in your refrigerator for convenient healthy snacks.

- **Whole grains**
  Explore your market for whole-grain products such as whole wheat and whole-grain breads and pastas, brown rice, bulgur, barley, cornmeal, whole wheat couscous, oats, farro, and quinoa to enjoy with your meals.

Read the recipe

Take a couple of minutes to read through the ingredients and directions before you start to prepare a recipe. This will prevent you from discovering midway through that you don't have an important ingredient or that a recipe requires several hours of marinating. It's also a good idea to assemble all ingredients and utensils within easy reach before you begin cooking.

Weighing and measuring

The success of any recipe depends on accurate weighing and measuring. The effectiveness of the Weight Watchers plan and the accuracy of the nutritional analysis depend on correct measuring as well. Use the following techniques:

- Weigh foods such as meat, poultry, and fish on a food scale.

- To measure liquids, use a standard glass or plastic measuring cup placed on a level surface. For amounts less than ¼ cup, use standard measuring spoons.

- To measure dry ingredients, use metal or plastic measuring cups that come in ¼-, ⅓-, ½-, and 1-cup sizes. Fill the appropriate cup and level it with the flat edge of a knife or spatula. For amounts less than ¼ cup, use standard measuring spoons.

Parmesan-basil broiled tomatoes, page 200

Introduction
What WW Freestyle is all about

Welcome to WW Freestyle! Our newest program makes deciding what to eat much easier, with dramatically less tracking, so you can focus on what really matters in your weight-loss journey—nourishing your whole self and doing more of the things that you enjoy.

How does it work?

The WW Freestyle program uses our incredibly effective SmartPoints system to guide you toward go-to foods that are the foundation of healthy eating.

- Every food is assigned a SmartPoints value, based on its nutrition.
- If the value is high, that means it is higher in sugar and saturated fat, and lower in protein, than some other foods.
- If the value is low, it is lower in sugar and saturated fat, and higher in protein.

All foods are yours for the eating and enjoying: You choose based on their SmartPoints value, your personalized SmartPoints Budget, and what you're in the mood for.

More freedom and flexibility

With WW Freestyle, you have a wide list of go-to foods that are zero Points! These zero Points foods include: chicken and turkey, seafood, plant-based proteins, eggs, veggies, unsweetened plain fat-free yogurt*, and fruits. These foods don't need to be tracked or measured so you can spend less time planning and counting, and more time enjoying food and your life. And you'll still lose weight!

That's where this book comes in

Every delicious recipe includes at least one (and sometimes many more!) zero Points foods, and every dish is full of flavor and designed to help you achieve success. Not only that, every dish can be prepared from start to finish in 30 minutes or less—and nearly half the recipes are ready in 20 minutes or less!

You'll also find "Eat better" tips for making the most of zero Points foods. And because successful members are the real experts, we've included some of their best ideas with "Let's do this together" tips.

Let's get cooking!

*When yogurt is used in these recipes we refer to it simply as plain, fat-free yogurt.

Add something extra

Now that so many foods are zero Points on WW Freestyle, you've probably got a few extra SmartPoints to play with! Here are some of our favorite flavor-packed foods to add great taste and variety to everyday eating.

Avocados

Creamy, rich, and flavorful, ripe avocado can stand in for mayo on a sandwich, get tossed into salads and salsas, or spread on toast for breakfast or a snack.

¼ Hass avocado
2 SmartPoints value

Bacon

Is there anything that doesn't taste better with bacon? We don't think so! Add a slice to a sandwich, crumble it into a casserole, sprinkle it over a salad, soup, or pasta dish, or enjoy it with your breakfast.

1 slice crisp cooked bacon
2 SmartPoints value

Butter

Nothing adds richness and flavor like butter. Toss it into plain cooked veggies, pasta, or rice; drizzle it over roasted fish or shrimp; add a bit to a pan sauce just before serving, or spread it on your morning toast.

1 teaspoon butter
2 SmartPoints value

Chocolate

Add a few shavings to a fruit salad, sprinkle it on bread and microwave for a few seconds to melt for a luxury snack or dessert, sprinkle it over a waffle or pancake, layer it into a yogurt and fruit parfait, or just savor a small chunk on its own!

½ ounce dark chocolate
4 SmartPoints value

Dried Fruits

When you're craving sweetness, but don't want to indulge in processed sugar, dried fruits can appease a sweet tooth. Keep a variety on hand for snacks and use them in salads, cereals and granola, pilafs, and curry dishes.

1 medium dried date
1 SmartPoints value

2 dried apricot halves
1 SmartPoints value

2 tablespoons dried cranberries or raisins
3 SmartPoints value

Honey

Need a bite of something sweet? Go for the real deal and swirl on natural honey. Varieties like clover, buckwheat, and orange blossom have different flavors, so experiment to find your favorite for drizzling onto toast, plain fat-free yogurt, oatmeal, fruit salads, or roasted vegetables (like Brussels sprouts, carrots, or butternut squash).

1 teaspoon honey
1 SmartPoints value

Nuts & Seeds

Add flavor and crunch to oatmeal, cereal, or soup with a few nuts or seeds (like pumpkin, sesame, or sunflower). They can dress up a yogurt and fruit snack or elevate an ordinary salad. And, of course, they're a must for pesto. Toast them first to intensify the flavor.

1 tablespoon almonds, sunflower seeds, or pumpkin seeds
1 SmartPoints value

1 tablespoon sesame seeds or walnuts
2 SmartPoints value

Cheeses

Go for bold-tasting cheeses so a small amount will add big flavor. A little bit of blue, feta, goat cheese, or Parmigiano-Reggiano can pump up the flavor of omelettes, soups, salads, casseroles, pasta dishes, and sandwiches.

1 tablespoon crumbled blue, feta, or goat cheese or grated Parmigiano-Reggiano
1 SmartPoints value

Olives

Use a few briny olives to upgrade the flavor of almost any dish. Chop them or cut them into slivers before adding to dips, salads, frittatas, pasta dishes, sandwich fillings, or pizza.

6 black or green olives
1 SmartPoints value

Flavorful oils

Choose oils like extra-virgin olive oil, Asian (dark) sesame oil, or roasted oils such as walnut or pumpkinseed to drizzle over plain chicken or fish, supercharge a salad dressing, boost the flavor of roasted or grilled vegetables, or toss with popcorn.

1 teaspoon any oil
1 SmartPoints value (except coconut oil is 2 SmartPoints value per teaspoon)

Butter

Dried apricots

Almonds

Dried dates

Avocado

Chocolate

Walnuts

Honey

Blue cheese

Dried cranberries

Sesame seeds

Parmigiano-Reggiano

Bacon

Pumpkin seeds

Sunflower seeds

Olive oil

Olives

Quick bbq
chicken breasts,
page 12

chapter 1
Protein-packed meals: chicken and turkey

How to cook perfectly moist, delicious chicken breasts

Boneless skinless chicken breasts: convenient, versatile, and able to go from fridge to table in a miraculous 10 minutes. They're a weeknight wonder, but how do you ensure that your chicken ends up juicy and flavorful, not chewy and bland?

Pan-searing is the answer. Searing creates a delicious crust on chicken as juices are pulled towards the surface and caramelize, giving you great texture, deep flavor, and fabulous aroma. Very little added fat is needed, and it's so speedy you'll want to have the table set before you start cooking. Here's how to make them perfect every time. And, FYI, this same technique works for turkey breast cutlets, too!

1 Start with breasts about 5 or 6 ounces each. If they're thicker than ¾ inch or very uneven in thickness, place them between two sheets of plastic wrap and pound them lightly with the bottom of a small heavy saucepan or rolling pin. Pat them dry with paper towels and season generously with salt and pepper.

2 Choose a heavy skillet that will hold your chicken in a single layer with enough space to turn them easily; an 8-inch skillet typically works for two breasts, and a 12-inch skillet is usually good for four.

3 Heat enough oil to just cover the bottom of the skillet over medium-high heat. When the oil is hot and almost shimmers, add the chicken. Let sit undisturbed for 1 minute, then give the skillet a firm shake by the handle to loosen the breasts (this will help them cook without sticking). Cook until the underside of the chicken is golden brown, about 3 to 4 minutes.

4 Flip the breasts with tongs and repeat on the other side. Test the chicken for doneness by using the tip of a paring knife to peek into the center of a breast; it will look moist and ivory-colored with no noticeable pink when it's done (and will register 165°F on an instant-read thermometer). If they need a few more minutes, lower the heat, cover the skillet, and test again in 2 minutes.

5 Transfer the chicken to plates or a platter. You can prepare a pan sauce in the same skillet (see recommendations opposite), or simply top the chicken with chopped fresh herbs, a sprinkle of coarse salt, and a squeeze of lemon—delicious!

Wine makes a flavorful ingredient as the base to a pan sauce.

Our favorite three-ingredient pan sauces
How easy can a sauce be? Very! Here's the basic method:

Return the same skillet to medium heat. Add an aromatic (usually some member of the onion family) and cook, scraping the bottom of the pan, until it's fragrant and softened. Stir in a liquid like broth or wine or a juicy fruit or vegetable like tomato or berries. Cook until reduced slightly, then stir in a final flavoring ingredient and season with salt and pepper. Pour over chicken breasts, adding a final garnish of herbs or cracked pepper if you like.

Pan sauces offer infinite room for experimentation, but here are some popular combos featuring ingredients you probably have on hand. The quantities below are for four servings.

Shallot + white wine + capers

1 minced shallot, ½ cup white wine, 2 tablespoons drained capers. 1 SmartPoints value per serving

Garlic + tomato + olives

4 minced garlic cloves, 1 diced tomato, 10 sliced pitted olives. 0 SmartPoints value per serving

Scallions + chicken broth + miso

3 chopped scallions, ½ cup chicken broth, 1 tablespoon miso paste. 0 SmartPoints value per serving

Fennel + orange + almonds

1 small chopped fennel bulb, 1 large peeled and chopped seedless orange, 2 tablespoons chopped almonds. 1 SmartPoints value per serving

Red onion + chicken broth + mustard

⅓ cup diced red onion, ½ cup chicken broth, 2 teaspoons Dijon or coarse-grained mustard. 0 SmartPoints value per serving

Chicken with strawberry-balsamic salsa

serves 4   gluten free   under 20 minutes

Although it can be prepared in 20 minutes or less, this recipe combines a variety of complex flavors that will surprise anyone you have over for dinner. The sweetness of the strawberries is complemented by the tart fruitiness and mellow flavor of the balsamic glaze, and jalapeño pepper turns up the heat. Depending on your taste, you can swap in mint or cilantro for the basil, though strawberry-basil is a classic combo we love!

4	**(5-ounce) skinless boneless chicken breast cutlets**
1	**teaspoon salt**
½	**teaspoon black pepper**
2	**cups hulled diced fresh strawberries**
3	**tablespoons balsamic glaze**
2	**tablespoons thinly sliced fresh basil**
2	**tablespoons thinly sliced scallions**
2	**teaspoons minced jalapeño pepper**

1 Spray ridged grill pan with nonstick spray and set over medium-high heat.

2 Sprinkle chicken with ½ teaspoon salt and ¼ teaspoon pepper. Place chicken in pan and grill, turning once, until chicken is cooked through, 8–10 minutes.

3 Meanwhile, to make salsa, combine strawberries, balsamic glaze, basil, scallions, jalapeño, remaining ½ teaspoon salt and remaining ¼ teaspoon pepper in medium bowl and stir gently to combine.

4 Serve chicken with salsa.

1 **SmartPoints value per serving** (1 chicken cutlet and ½ cup salsa): 212 Cal, 4 g Total Fat, 1 g Sat Fat, 646 mg Sod, 10 g Total Carb, 7 g Sugar, 2 g Fib, 32 g Prot.

Chicken with strawberry-balsamic salsa

Grilled chicken with Indian spices

serves 4   gluten free

Who doesn't like grilled chicken, especially when you layer in the bold flavors of India. Choosing a spice paste to flavor grilled foods minimizes burning while maximizing flavor. Unlike thick barbecue sauces, which drip into the coals and invite flare-ups, this tangy mixture of lime, olive oil, paprika, and ginger infuses a spicy and aromatic note to chicken. When grilling, rotate chicken in and out of the hottest parts of the fire to ensure even cooking.

4 **scallions, sliced, plus additional sliced scallions for garnish**

½ **cup packed fresh cilantro leaves**

4 **garlic cloves, peeled**

Grated zest and juice of 1 lime

4 **teaspoons olive oil**

2 **teaspoons ground cumin**

1 **teaspoon paprika**

1 **teaspoon grated peeled fresh ginger**

4 **(5-ounce) skinless boneless chicken breast cutlets**

½ **teaspoon salt**

¼ **teaspoon black pepper**

Lime wedges

1 Spray grill rack with nonstick spray. Preheat grill to medium or prepare medium fire.

2 Combine 4 scallions, cilantro, garlic, lime zest and juice, oil, cumin, paprika, and ginger in mini-food processor and process until coarse paste forms. Rub paste all over chicken. Let stand 10 minutes.

3 Place chicken on grill rack and grill, turning occasionally, until chicken is cooked through, about 10 minutes. Sprinkle with salt and pepper. Arrange chicken on platter and garnish with remaining scallions and lime wedges.

1 **SmartPoints value per serving** (1 chicken cutlet): 229 Cal, 9 g Total Fat, 1 g Sat Fat, 360 mg Sod, 5 g Total Carb, 1 g Sugar, 1 g Fib, 32 g Prot.

Eat better
The secret to moist and tender grilled chicken breasts is to cook them just until they are done to prevent them from becoming tough and dry. Check for doneness often and remove the chicken from the grill as soon as it is cooked through.

Chicken with quinoa and roasted carrots

serves 4   gluten free

Quinoa, although cooked as a grain like rice, is actually a seed. In this recipe, we flavor quinoa with cumin and lemon zest and serve it as a side to grilled chicken. Spinach, mint, and carrots add vibrant color to the plate. We love this dish because it's hearty, nurturing, and warm— all that we desire on a wintery night.

⅔ **cup quinoa**

1   **cup chicken broth**

2   **large carrots, thinly sliced on diagonal**

4   **teaspoons honey**

2   **teaspoons ground cumin**

¾   **teaspoon salt**

1   **teaspoon paprika**

¼   **teaspoon black pepper**

4   **(5-ounce) skinless boneless chicken breast cutlets**

Grated zest and juice of 1 small lemon

1   **tablespoon extra-virgin olive oil**

2   **cups baby spinach**

½   **cup fresh mint leaves, chopped**

2   **tablespoons pistachios, coarsely chopped**

1 Adjust oven racks to divide oven into thirds; preheat oven to 425°F. Line small rimmed baking sheet with parchment paper.

2 Place quinoa in small saucepan and set over medium-high heat. Cook, stirring frequently, until fragrant, about 5 minutes. Stir in broth and bring to boil. Reduce heat to low and simmer, covered, until liquid is absorbed and quinoa is tender, about 20 minutes.

3 Meanwhile, combine carrots, 2 teaspoons honey, 1 teaspoon cumin, and ⅛ teaspoon salt in medium bowl. Spread carrots on baking sheet. Roast carrots on lowest oven rack until browned and tender, about 15 minutes.

4 Stir together remaining 1 teaspoon cumin, paprika, ½ teaspoon salt, and pepper in small dish. Rub spice mixture on both sides of chicken. Spray chicken with olive oil nonstick spray. Heat ridged grill pan over medium-high heat until hot. Place chicken in pan and grill, turning once, until chicken is cooked through, 8–10 minutes. Transfer chicken to cutting board and thinly slice.

5 To make dressing, whisk together lemon zest and juice, oil, remaining 2 teaspoons honey, and remaining ⅛ teaspoon salt in small bowl. Fluff quinoa with fork; transfer to large bowl. Add spinach, mint, carrots, and 3 tablespoons dressing; toss to coat. Divide quinoa mixture among 4 plates; top evenly with chicken, pistachios, and remaining 1 tablespoon dressing.

6 **SmartPoints value per serving** (1 chicken cutlet and ¾ cup quinoa mixture): 389 Cal, 11 g Total Fat, 2 g Sat Fat, 729 mg Sod, 33 g Total Carb, 9 g Sugar, 5 g Fib, 39 g Prot.

**Paprika chicken
with orange-olive
relish**

Paprika chicken with orange-olive relish

serves 4   **gluten free**   **under 20 minutes**

When you're short on time, this is a dish you can whip up in a flash: While the chicken is cooking, quickly prepare a sauce that features Peppadew peppers. Peppadew is the trademarked brand name of a sweet pepper from South Africa that was not discovered until 1993. Nevertheless, it has found its place on menus everywhere and in this relish, which is a classic mix of sweet and sour.

1   **teaspoon smoked paprika**

¾   **teaspoon salt**

¼   **teaspoon black pepper**

4   **(5-ounce) skinless boneless chicken breast cutlets**

2   **large navel oranges, peeled, sectioned, and roughly chopped**

4   **large green olives, pitted and coarsely chopped**

4   **Peppadew peppers, drained and chopped**

2   **tablespoons chopped fresh flat-leaf parsley**

1   **tablespoon extra-virgin olive oil**

2   **teaspoons red-wine vinegar**

1   Stir together paprika, ½ teaspoon salt, and pepper in cup. Rub spice mixture all over chicken.

2   Heat ridged grill pan over medium-high heat until hot. Spray chicken with olive oil nonstick spray. Place chicken in pan and grill, turning once, until chicken is cooked through, 8–10 minutes.

3   Meanwhile, to make relish, combine oranges, olives, Peppadew peppers, parsley, oil, vinegar, and remaining ¼ teaspoon salt in medium bowl. Serve chicken with relish.

1 **SmartPoints value per serving** (1 chicken cutlet and about ⅓ cup relish): 255 Cal, 8 g Total Fat, 1 g Sat Fat, 710 mg Sod, 12 g Total Carb, 9 g Sugar, 3 g Fib, 33 g Prot.

Let's do this together

Dishes like this one save time by doing double duty as an instant lunch the next day. As Weight Watchers member Michael Hamlin says: "Leftovers are great because I've already figured out the SmartPoints value the night before!"

Chicken with apricots and sage

serves 4   gluten free   under 20 minutes

While wonderful eaten fresh, apricots also make a fine accoutrement for chicken. Here, they are introduced into the dish two ways: dried and as a fruit spread. The pan sauce is made to accentuate the flavor of the apricots; when cooking them with the brandy, be sure to scrape up the tasty bits that stick to the pan. Finish by adding sage, lemon juice, and a bit of butter for an irresistibly luxurious sauce.

3	teaspoons olive oil
4	(5-ounce) skinless boneless chicken breast cutlets
½	teaspoon salt
¼	teaspoon black pepper
2	shallots, finely chopped
¼	cup dried apricots, diced
2	tablespoons brandy
⅔	cup chicken broth
2	tablespoons all-fruit apricot spread
2	teaspoons butter
2	teaspoons chopped fresh sage
1	teaspoon lemon juice

1 Heat 2 teaspoons oil in large skillet over medium-high heat. Sprinkle chicken with salt and pepper. Add chicken and cook, turning once, until cooked through, 8–10 minutes. Transfer chicken to plate and keep warm.

2 Heat remaining 1 teaspoon oil in same skillet over medium heat. Add shallots and apricots; cook, stirring frequently, until shallots soften, about 2 minutes. Add brandy and cook until liquid evaporates, about 30 seconds. Stir in broth and apricot spread; increase heat and cook, scraping up browned bits from bottom of pan, until slightly thickened, 2–3 minutes.

3 Remove pan from heat; add butter, sage, and lemon juice, stirring until butter melts. Return chicken and any accumulated juices to skillet; turn chicken to coat with sauce.

(5) **SmartPoints value per serving** (1 chicken cutlet and about 3 tablespoons sauce): 288 Cal, 9 g Total Fat, 3 g Sat Fat, 481 mg Sod, 13 g Total Carb, 10 g Sugar, 1 g Fib, 33 g Prot.

Eat better

Look for USDA certified organic chicken at the supermarket. It costs a little more, but it's worth it to know that the chicken was raised under humane conditions and fed an organic diet.

Chicken salad with cucumber-yogurt sauce

serves 4   under 20 minutes

1   **pound chicken breast tenders**
2   **tablespoons white-wine vinegar**
2   **large garlic cloves, minced**
1   **teaspoon dried oregano**
1   **teaspoon salt**
¼   **teaspoon plus ⅛ teaspoon black pepper**
¾   **cup plain fat-free yogurt**
¾   **cup finely diced English (seedless) cucumber**
4   **tablespoons chopped fresh mint**
2   **tablespoons chopped fresh dill**
½   **teaspoon ground cumin**
4   **teaspoons olive oil**
2   **cups thinly sliced romaine lettuce**
1   **large tomato, diced**
½   **cup thinly sliced red onion**
2   **(6-inch) pita breads, toasted and cut into wedges**

1   Combine chicken, vinegar, garlic, oregano, ¾ teaspoon salt, and ¼ teaspoon pepper in large bowl; stir until mixed well. Let stand 10 minutes.

2   Meanwhile, to make yogurt sauce, stir together yogurt, cucumber, 2 tablespoons mint, dill, cumin, remaining ¼ teaspoon salt, and remaining ⅛ teaspoon pepper in small bowl.

3   Heat oil in large nonstick skillet over medium heat. Add chicken and cook until browned and cooked through, about 2 minutes per side. Transfer chicken to plate and let cool slightly.

4   Divide lettuce among 4 plates; top evenly with chicken, tomato, onion, and yogurt sauce. Sprinkle with remaining 2 tablespoons mint. Serve with pita wedges.

 2   **SmartPoints value per serving** (3 chicken tenders, ¼ of salad, ¼ cup sauce, and ½ pita bread): 266 Cal, 8 g Total Fat, 1 g Sat Fat, 747 mg Sod, 17 g Total Carb, 6 g Sugar, 2 g Fib, 31 g Prot.

Eat better
Chicken breast tenders are strips of meat attached to the underside of a chicken breast, and they are the same white meat as the breast—and zero Points on the WW Freestyle program.

Quick bbq chicken breasts

serves 6   **gluten free**   **under 20 minutes**

The basic ingredients in a barbecue sauce are pretty simple: a generous dose of ketchup, smaller amounts of vinegar, and a selection of flavorings. Here we use apple cider vinegar and brown sugar to develop a rich, complex flavor; cumin and paprika add a twist to what you'd find in a traditional barbecue sauce. For this recipe, you separate the dry rub and the liquid glaze, which helps you avoid any burning or flare-ups while still delivering all the flavor you'd expect. And best of all, it takes only 10 minutes to cook.

¼   **cup ketchup**

2   **tablespoons apple cider vinegar**

1½   **tablespoons packed brown sugar**

2   **garlic cloves, minced**

1½   **teaspoons smoked paprika**

1½   **teaspoons ground cumin**

¾   **teaspoon salt**

¼   **teaspoon black pepper**

6   **(5-ounce) skinless boneless chicken breast cutlets**

1 Spray grill rack with nonstick spray. Preheat grill to medium or prepare medium fire.

2 To make glaze, stir together ketchup, vinegar, brown sugar, and garlic in small bowl.

3 To make spice rub, mix together paprika, cumin, salt, and pepper in another small bowl. Rub spice mixture all over chicken.

4 Place chicken on grill rack and grill, turning often, until cooked through, about 10 minutes. Brush chicken on both sides with glaze and grill 1 minute longer.

1 **SmartPoints value per serving** (1 chicken cutlet): 198 Cal, 4 g Total Fat, 1 g Sat Fat, 447 mg Sod, 7 g Total Carb, 6 g Sugar, 0 g Fib, 32 g Prot.

Let's do this together

Take an idea from member Kate Leissler and double up on this recipe. "I cook a ton of chicken," she explains. "I use it throughout the week for tacos, salads, and sandwiches."

Chicken and kale salad with miso dressing

Chicken and kale salad with miso dressing

serves 4   under 20 minutes

This recipe is a Japanese take on chicken breast with green vegetables. Here we opt for kale, though you can use spinach or Asian blend salad greens instead. While the chicken is grilling, make the dressing: Its outrageously delicious salty-sweet flavor comes from a one-two punch of miso, a paste made from fermented soybeans, and mirin, a sweet Japanese rice vinegar. Ginger and pepper flakes give the dressing spice and heat.

4   **(5-ounce) skinless boneless chicken breast cutlets**
¾   **teaspoon salt**
¼   **teaspoon black pepper**
2   **tablespoons mirin**
4   **teaspoons rice vinegar**
1   **tablespoon white or yellow miso**
1   **teaspoon grated peeled fresh ginger**
Pinch red pepper flakes
6   **cups baby kale**
2   **carrots, shredded**
4   **large radishes, halved and thinly sliced**

1 Heat ridged grill pan over medium-high heat until hot. Sprinkle chicken with ½ teaspoon salt and black pepper. Spray chicken with olive oil nonstick spray. Place chicken in pan and grill, turning once, until chicken is cooked through, 8–10 minutes.

2 Meanwhile, to make dressing, whisk together mirin, vinegar, miso, ginger, pepper flakes and remaining ¼ teaspoon salt in small bowl.

3 Place kale, carrots, and radishes in large bowl; add 2 tablespoons dressing and toss to coat.

4 Divide kale mixture evenly among 4 plates. Top each serving with 1 chicken cutlet. Drizzle chicken with remaining dressing.

0 **SmartPoints value per serving** (1 chicken cutlet, 1¼ cups kale mixture, and about 1½ teaspoons dressing): 209 Cal, 4 g Total Fat, 1 g Sat Fat, 709 mg Sod, 7 g Total Carb, 3 g Sugar, 2 g Fib, 34 g Prot.

Let's do this together
Speed up shopping by ordering online and picking up your order at the grocery store. Weight Watchers member Brandy Evans says: "This has revolutionized grocery shopping particularly during those weeks when I simply can't figure out how to squeeze one more thing in."

Chicken sandwiches with avocado "mayo"

serves 4   under 20 minutes

Chicken breast cutlets, which are thinner than regular chicken breasts, are perfect for this recipe. Make a guacamole-type spread with avocado, jalapeño, lime zest, and lime juice, then sprinkle hearty slices of tomatoes lightly with salt and pepper. Voilà—you have the makings of the ultimate chicken sandwich. Slather slices of toasted whole wheat bread with avocado mayo, layer in tomatoes garnished with cilantro, top with Bibb lettuce, and add the chicken breast hot off the grill pan.

1	**pound skinless boneless chicken breast cutlets**
¾	**teaspoon plus ⅛ teaspoon salt**
½	**teaspoon chili powder**
1	**ripe avocado, pitted and peeled**
1	**jalapeño pepper, seeded and minced**
1	**teaspoon grated lime zest**
1	**teaspoon lime juice**
2	**tomatoes, sliced**
⅛	**teaspoon black pepper**
8	**slices whole wheat country bread, toasted**
¼	**cup minced fresh cilantro**
	Bibb lettuce leaves

1 Spray large ridged grill pan with nonstick spray and set over medium-high heat. Sprinkle chicken with ½ teaspoon salt and chili powder. Add chicken to pan and cook, turning once, until cooked through, about 8 minutes.

2 Meanwhile, place avocado in medium bowl and mash using fork. Stir in jalapeño, lime zest and juice, and ¼ teaspoon salt.

3 Sprinkle tomatoes with remaining ⅛ teaspoon salt and black pepper.

4 Spread one side of 4 bread slices evenly with avocado mixture; top evenly with tomatoes. Sprinkle tomatoes with cilantro; top with chicken, lettuce, and remaining bread slices.

7 **SmartPoints value per serving** (1 sandwich): 394 Cal, 12 g Total Fat, 2 g Sat Fat, 868 mg Sod, 35 g Total Carb, 5 g Sugar, 8 g Fib, 35 g Prot.

Chicken sandwiches with avocado "mayo"

Chicken with fresh tomato–balsamic sauce

Chicken with fresh tomato–balsamic sauce

serves 4   gluten free   under 20 minutes

Pairing rosemary and chicken is like pairing tomato and basil: Both are exquisite matches that are easy for home cooks to master. Here we scatter fresh rosemary on chicken cutlets and cook them quickly in olive oil. After removing the chicken, we sauté shallots, then garlic, and then add balsamic vinegar to the saucepan, scraping up any bits of meat stuck on the bottom of the pan—this is where all the flavor lies. We amp up the sauce with a robust balance of sweet tomatoes and briny capers.

4	**(¼-pound) thin-sliced skinless boneless chicken cutlets**
2	**teaspoons chopped fresh rosemary**
½	**teaspoon salt**
¼	**teaspoon black pepper**
2	**teaspoons olive oil**
2	**shallots, thinly sliced**
2	**garlic cloves, minced**
2	**tablespoons balsamic vinegar**
2	**cups red or yellow cherry tomatoes (or mix of both), halved**
¼	**cup chicken broth**
2	**teaspoons drained capers**
1	**tablespoon grated lemon zest**

1 Sprinkle chicken with ½ teaspoon rosemary, ¼ teaspoon salt, and pepper. Heat oil in large skillet over medium-high heat. Add chicken and cook just until browned and cooked through, 2–3 minutes per side. Transfer chicken to platter and keep warm.

2 Add shallots and garlic to same skillet; cook over medium heat, stirring, until softened, about 2 minutes. Add vinegar; cook, stirring with wooden spoon and scraping up any browned bits from bottom of pan, until vinegar evaporates.

3 Stir in tomatoes, broth, capers, lemon zest, remaining 1½ teaspoons rosemary, and remaining ¼ teaspoon salt. Cook, stirring frequently, until tomatoes are softened, about 3 minutes. Return chicken and any accumulated juices to skillet; heat through.

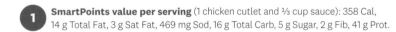

1 **SmartPoints value per serving** (1 chicken cutlet and ⅓ cup sauce): 358 Cal, 14 g Total Fat, 3 g Sat Fat, 469 mg Sod, 16 g Total Carb, 5 g Sugar, 2 g Fib, 41 g Prot.

Eat better
Thin-sliced chicken cutlets cook faster and offer a smaller portion than regular skinless boneless chicken breasts. You can buy them or make your own by cutting a regular chicken breast in half horizontally.

Chicken satay with red curry–peanut sauce

serves 4

Peanut powder is made by roasting peanuts, then squeezing out the oil and grinding the remaining peanut mixture into a fine powder. At just 1 SmartPoints value for 2 tablespoons (compared to 6 SmartPoints value for 2 tablespoons of regular peanut butter), it's a great way to add peanut flavor to sauces, smoothies, baked goods, and even oatmeal.

¼ **cup light (low-fat) coconut milk**

¼ **cup peanut powder**

2 **tablespoons soy sauce**

1 **tablespoon grated peeled fresh ginger**

1 **tablespoon packed brown sugar**

½ **teaspoon Thai red curry paste**

1 **tablespoon chopped fresh cilantro**

1 **pound skinless boneless chicken breast, cut into 1½-inch pieces**

1 **red bell pepper, cut into 2-inch pieces**

1 **yellow bell pepper, cut into 2-inch pieces**

4 **scallions, cut into 3-inch lengths**

½ **teaspoon salt**

1 Spray grill rack with nonstick spray. Preheat grill to medium high or prepare medium-hot fire.

2 Meanwhile, to make sauce, combine coconut milk, peanut powder, soy sauce, ginger, brown sugar, and curry paste in small saucepan and set over medium heat. Cook, stirring constantly, until mixture is smooth and heated through, about 3 minutes. Remove saucepan from heat and stir in cilantro. Transfer to serving bowl and set aside.

3 Thread chicken, peppers, and scallions alternately on 4 (10-inch) metal skewers. Sprinkle with salt. Place skewers on grill rack and grill, turning occasionally, until chicken is cooked through andvegetables are tender, 10–12 minutes. Serve with peanut sauce.

2 **SmartPoints value per serving** (1 skewer and 3 tablespoons sauce): 206 Cal, 5 g Total Fat, 1 g Sat Fat, 837 mg Sod, 11 g Total Carb, 6 g Sugar, 3 g Fib, 30 g Prot.

Curried chicken with apple and mango

serves 4   gluten free

Curry dishes like this one taste only as good as the curry powder you use. If you're a fan of curry, seek out a curry powder blend from a good-quality brand—it really makes a difference in the flavor of the finished dish. One brand we like is Frontier.

2	**teaspoons canola oil**
1	**pound skinless boneless chicken breast, cut into 2-inch pieces**
½	**teaspoon salt**
¼	**teaspoon black pepper**
1	**small Granny Smith apple, unpeeled, cored and diced**
1	**small onion, chopped**
1½	**teaspoons grated peeled fresh ginger**
1	**garlic clove, minced**
2	**teaspoons curry powder**
3	**tablespoons currants**
¼	**cup chicken broth**
¼	**cup fat-free half-and-half**
⅓	**cup mango chutney**
2	**tablespoons slivered almonds, toasted**
1	**tablespoon chopped fresh cilantro or basil**

1 Heat oil in large nonstick skillet over medium heat. Sprinkle chicken with salt and pepper; add to skillet and cook, turning occasionally, until cooked through, about 6 minutes. Transfer to plate.

2 Add apple, onion, ginger, and garlic to skillet. Cook until apple and onion are tender, about 6 minutes. Stir in curry powder; cook 1 minute. Add chicken, currants, broth, and half-and-half; bring to boil. Simmer, uncovered, until sauce thickens slightly, about 3 minutes. Stir in chutney. Sprinkle with almonds and cilantro.

(4) **SmartPoints value per serving** (1 cup): 250 Cal, 8 g Total Fat, 1 g Sat Fat, 459 mg Sod, 18 g Total Carb, 12 g Sugar, 3 g Fib, 28 g Prot.

Lemon-basil chicken-and-vegetable kebabs

serves 4   gluten free

As an alternative to the kebabs, you can make this dish quicker by grilling the chicken breasts whole and placing the veggies in a grill basket to cook. Either way, simple cooked couscous (at 2 SmartPoints value per ½ cup) makes an easy side dish.

Grated zest and juice from 1 large lemon

4   teaspoons canola oil

3   garlic cloves, minced

½   teaspoon salt

¼   teaspoon black pepper

1   pound skinless boneless chicken breast, cut into cubes

1   zucchini, halved lengthwise and sliced

1   yellow squash, halved lengthwise and sliced

1   pint cherry tomatoes

1   red onion, cut into 8 wedges

¼   cup chopped fresh basil

Lemon wedges

1 Spray grill rack with nonstick spray; preheat grill to medium high or prepare medium-hot fire.

2 Stir together lemon zest and juice, oil, garlic, salt, and pepper in large bowl; add chicken, zucchini, yellow squash, tomatoes, and onion; toss to coat. Thread onto 16 (6-inch) skewers. (If using wooden skewers, soak in water 30 minutes before threading on chicken and vegetables.)

3 Place skewers on grill rack and grill, turning frequently, until browned and cooked through, 10–12 minutes. Transfer to serving platter and sprinkle with basil. Serve with lemon wedges.

① SmartPoints value per serving (4 kebabs): 229 Cal, 8 g Total Fat, 1 g Sat Fat, 355 mg Sod, 12 g Total Carb, 6 g Sugar, 3 g Fib, 28 g Prot.

Lemon-basil chicken-and-vegetable kebabs

**Chicken and broccoli
slaw with cashews**

Chicken and broccoli slaw with cashews

serves 4   under 20 minutes

Seasoned rice vinegar is plain rice vinegar that has sugar and salt added. If you only have regular rice vinegar on hand, taste this dish before serving—it might need a pinch of salt or sugar. Cashews add a delicious crunch to the salad, but peanuts or almonds would taste great, too.

2	tablespoons seasoned rice vinegar
1½	tablespoons soy sauce
1	tablespoon mirin
1	teaspoon minced peeled fresh ginger
1	teaspoon Asian (dark) sesame oil
¼	teaspoon red pepper flakes
¾	pound skinless boneless chicken breast, cut into 1-inch pieces
¼	teaspoon salt
1	(12-ounce) package broccoli slaw mix
1	red bell pepper, thinly sliced
½	cup chopped fresh cilantro
2	scallions, finely chopped
¼	cup coarsely chopped unsalted cashews

1 To make dressing, whisk together vinegar, soy sauce, mirin, ginger, oil, and pepper flakes in small bowl until blended; set aside.

2 Spray large skillet with nonstick spray and set over medium-high heat. Sprinkle chicken with salt. Add chicken to skillet and cook, turning occasionally, until cooked through, about 8 minutes.

3 Combine broccoli slaw, bell pepper, cilantro, and scallions in large bowl; add dressing and toss well to coat.

4 Add chicken to slaw mixture and toss lightly. Divide slaw evenly among 4 plates and serve sprinkled with cashews.

2 **SmartPoints value per serving** (1½ cups slaw and 1 tablespoon cashews): 201 Cal, 7 g Total Fat, 1 g Sat Fat, 539 mg Sod, 10 g Total Carb, 3 g Sugar, 4 g Fib, 23 g Prot.

Asian chicken wraps with mango

serves 4

Instead of using the chicken mixture for wraps, you can serve it as a warm salad on top of spinach or lettuce, or serve it over cooked spiralized vegetable "noodles," rice noodles, or soba noodles. Any leftovers make a delicious lunch to pack for work later in the week.

1	**pound boneless skinless chicken breast, cut into ½-inch cubes**
2	**tablespoons all-purpose flour**
¼	**teaspoon salt**
4	**teaspoons Asian (dark) sesame oil**
3	**tablespoons soy sauce**
3	**tablespoons unseasoned rice vinegar**
2	**scallions, thinly sliced**
3	**garlic cloves, minced**
1	**tablespoon minced peeled fresh ginger**
1	**ripe mango, peeled, pitted, and chopped**
2	**tablespoons chopped fresh mint or cilantro**
8	**large Bibb lettuce leaves**
¼	**cup roasted salted peanuts, finely chopped**

Lime wedges

1 Place chicken in medium bowl; add flour and salt and toss to coat.

2 Heat 2 teaspoons oil in large nonstick skillet over medium heat. Add chicken in batches and stir-fry until lightly browned, about 5 minutes. Transfer chicken to plate.

3 Meanwhile, stir together soy sauce and vinegar in small bowl. Set aside.

4 Add remaining 2 teaspoons oil to skillet. Add scallions, garlic, and ginger and stir-fry until fragrant, about 1 minute. Add soy sauce mixture and chicken and stir-fry until chicken is cooked through, about 1 minute. Stir in mango and remove from heat. Stir in mint.

5 Fill lettuce leaves evenly with chicken mixture and sprinkle with peanuts. Serve with lime wedges; roll up and eat out of hand.

3 **SmartPoints value per serving** (2 wraps): 294 Cal, 10 g Total Fat, 2 g Sat Fat, 938 mg Sod, 21 g Total Carb, 12 g Sugar, 3 g Fib, 30 g Prot.

Asian chicken
wraps with mango

Harissa turkey cutlets with warm bulgur salad

serves 4

Harissa is an aromatic paste of smoked hot peppers, garlic, olive oil, and spices widely used in North African and Middle Eastern cuisine. Look for it in the condiments aisle at the supermarket.

1½ cups water

1 teaspoon ground cumin

¾ teaspoon salt

¾ cup bulgur

3 tablespoons lemon juice

3 teaspoons olive oil

2 teaspoons harissa

4 (5-ounce) turkey breast cutlets

1 teaspoon grated lemon zest

1 large carrot, shredded

⅓ cup coarsely chopped fresh flat-leaf parsley

2 scallions, thinly sliced

2 tablespoons golden raisins, coarsely chopped

1 Combine water, cumin, and ¼ teaspoon salt in small saucepan. Bring to boil over high heat. Stir in bulgur. Reduce heat to low, cover, and simmer until liquid is absorbed and bulgur is tender, about 15 minutes.

2 Meanwhile, combine 1 tablespoon lemon juice, 2 teaspoons oil, and harissa in medium bowl. Add turkey and toss to coat. Let stand 10 minutes.

3 Spray ridged grill pan with nonstick spray and heat overmedium-high heat until hot. Place turkey in pan and grill, turning once, until turkey is cooked through, 8–10 minutes.

4 Fluff bulgur with fork. Whisk together remaining 2 tablespoons lemon juice, lemon zest, remaining 1 teaspoon oil, and remaining ½ teaspoon salt in large bowl. Add bulgur, carrot, parsley, scallions, and raisins; toss to coat. Serve with turkey.

4 **SmartPoints value per serving** (1 turkey cutlet and about ¾ cup salad): 312 Cal, 7 g Total Fat, 1 g Sat Fat, 468 mg Sod, 28 g Total Carb, 4 g Sugar, 4 g Fib, 37 g Prot.

Turkey with spinach-fennel rice

serves 4   gluten free   under 20 minutes

Look for ready-cooked brown rice in plastic packages near the dry rice at the supermarket. Some grocers also sell it in their store-made packaged foods section; or you can also pick up some at a Chinese restaurant.

2	teaspoons grated lemon zest
1	teaspoon dried oregano
¾	teaspoon salt
½	teaspoon black pepper
4	(5-ounce) turkey breast cutlets
1	tablespoon olive oil
1	small fennel bulb, thinly sliced
2	garlic cloves, minced
1	(8.8-ounce) package ready-cooked brown rice
2	cups firmly packed baby spinach
⅓	cup chopped fresh mint
3	tablespoons lemon juice
Lemon wedges	

1 Combine lemon zest, oregano, ½ teaspoon salt, and ¼ teaspoon black pepper in cup. Rub lemon mixture all over turkey. Spray turkey with olive oil nonstick spray.

2 Heat ridged grill pan over medium-high heat until hot. Place turkey in pan and grill, turning once, until turkey is cooked through, 8–10 minutes.

3 Meanwhile, heat oil in large skillet over medium-high heat. Add fennel, remaining ¼ teaspoon salt and remaining ¼ teaspoon pepper. Cook, stirring often, until crisp-tender, 2–3 minutes. Add garlic and cook, stirring constantly, until fragrant, about 30 seconds. Add rice and cook, stirring often, until heated through, about 2 minutes. Stir in spinach and cook until spinach wilts, about 1 minute.

4 Remove pan from heat and stir in mint and lemon juice. Serve turkey with rice and lemon wedges.

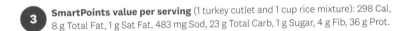

(3) **SmartPoints value per serving** (1 turkey cutlet and 1 cup rice mixture): 298 Cal, 8 g Total Fat, 1 g Sat Fat, 483 mg Sod, 23 g Total Carb, 1 g Sugar, 4 g Fib, 36 g Prot.

Turkey salad with
passion fruit dressing

Turkey salad with passion fruit dressing

serves 4   gluten free   under 20 minutes

Passion fruit is a deep purple egg-shaped fruit whose skin becomes dimpled when ripe. The pulp is golden with a jellylike consistency and contains edible black seeds. If you can't find passion fruit, you can substitute pureed mango in this recipe.

¼   **cup fresh or thawed frozen passion fruit pulp (about 4 passion fruits)**

2   **tablespoons orange juice**

2   **teaspoons plus 1 tablespoon extra-virgin olive oil**

1   **tablespoon lime juice**

1   **tablespoon honey**

½   **teaspoon salt**

⅛   **teaspoon plus ¼ teaspoon black pepper**

Pinch cayenne

1   **large egg white**

1   **tablespoon water**

⅓   **cup yellow cornmeal**

3   **tablespoons grated Parmesan**

4   **(5-ounce) turkey breast cutlets**

6   **ounces mixed baby greens (6 lightly packed cups)**

1 To make dressing, whisk together passion fruit pulp, orange juice, 2 teaspoons oil, lime juice, honey, ¼ teaspoon salt, ⅛ teaspoon pepper, and cayenne in large bowl until blended; set aside.

2 Whisk together egg white and water in large shallow bowl. Mix together cornmeal, Parmesan, remaining ¼ teaspoon salt, and remaining ¼ teaspoon pepper on sheet of wax paper.

3 Dip each cutlet into egg-white mixture, then coat with cornmeal mixture, pressing lightly so it adheres.

4 Heat remaining 1 tablespoon oil in large skillet over medium-high heat. Add cutlets and cook until browned and cooked through, about 3 minutes per side.

5 Add greens to dressing; toss until coated evenly. Transfer 1 cutlet to each of 4 plates. Top evenly with salad.

5 **SmartPoints value per serving** (1 turkey cutlet and about 1 cup salad): 288 Cal, 10 g Total Fat, 2 g Sat Fat, 394 mg Sod, 21 g Total Carb, 7 g Sugar, 3 g Fib, 31 g Prot.

Parmesan-crusted turkey with green salad

serves 4

2   **tablespoons whole wheat flour**

¼   **teaspoon plus ⅛ teaspoon salt**

1   **large egg white**

2   **teaspoons water**

3   **tablespoons whole wheat panko (bread crumbs)**

3   **tablespoons grated Parmesan**

4   **(5-ounce) turkey breast cutlets**

1   **teaspoon plus 1 tablespoon extra-virgin olive oil**

1   **tablespoon minced fresh chives**

1   **tablespoon red-wine vinegar**

½   **teaspoon Dijon mustard**

¼   **teaspoon black pepper**

1   **(5-ounce) container baby greens**

Pepperoncini and green tomato wedges, for garnish (optional)

1 Mix flour and ¼ teaspoon salt on sheet of wax paper. Beat together egg white and 1 teaspoon water in shallow dish. Combine panko and Parmesan on another sheet of wax paper. Working with 1 cutlet at a time, dip both sides into flour mixture. Dip into egg-white mixture and then panko mixture, pressing so it adheres.

2 Heat 1 teaspoon oil in large nonstick skillet over medium heat. Add turkey and cook until golden brown and cooked through, 4–5 minutes on each side.

3 Meanwhile, whisk together remaining 1 tablespoon oil, remaining 1 teaspoon water, chives, vinegar, mustard, pepper, and remaining ⅛ teaspoon salt in large bowl. Add greens; toss to coat. Serve turkey topped with salad. Garnish with pepperoncini and tomato wedges, if desired.

3 **SmartPoints value per serving** (1 turkey cutlet and about 1 cup salad): 235 Cal, 9 g Total Fat, 2 g Sat Fat, 354 mg Sod, 8 g Total Carb, 1 g Sugar, 2 g Fib, 31 g Prot.

Eat better

Add halved cherry tomatoes and sliced mini-cucumbers to the salad to pump up the crunch.

Parmesan-crusted turkey with green salad

**Turkey cutlets with
cranberry-pear chutney**

Turkey cutlets with cranberry-pear chutney

serves 4   gluten free   under 20 minutes

¼   cup chicken broth

3   tablespoons packed light
     brown sugar

3   tablespoons apple cider vinegar

2   tablespoons orange juice

¼   teaspoon cinnamon

¼   teaspoon ground ginger

Pinch ground cloves

4   (5-ounce) turkey breast cutlets

½   teaspoon salt

¼   teaspoon coarsely ground
     black pepper

1   teaspoon canola oil

1   ripe pear, peeled and chopped

1   cup fresh or frozen cranberries

1 Whisk together broth, brown sugar, vinegar, orange juice, cinnamon, ginger, and cloves in small bowl; set aside.

2 Sprinkle cutlets with salt and pepper. Heat oil in large skillet over medium-high heat. Add cutlets and cook until cooked through, about 3 minutes on each side. Transfer to plate and keep warm.

3 Add pear, cranberries, and broth mixture to same skillet; bring to boil. Simmer, uncovered, until berries begin to pop and chutney thickens, about 5 minutes. Serve chutney with cutlets.

3 **SmartPoints value per serving** (1 turkey cutlet and about ½ cup chutney): 253 Cal, 5 g Total Fat, 1 g Sat Fat, 329 mg Sod, 21 g Total Carb, 16 g Sugar, 3 g Fib, 34 g Prot.

Let's do this together

This saucy dish is so flavorful that you only need a simple side dish to serve alongside. Quick cooking veggies that can be microwaved or steamed are favorites of Weight Watchers member Kam Szabo. "We always have broccoli and carrots in the fridge and potatoes in the pantry, since they go with anything!"

Turkey soba soup

serves 4   under 20 minutes

2   teaspoons canola oil

3   (¼-pound) turkey breast cutlets, cut into thin strips

1   garlic clove, minced

4   cups reduced-sodium chicken broth

1   cup water

4   ounces soba noodles

½   pound baby bok choy, cut into 2-inch slices

3   scallions, thinly sliced

½   cup chopped fresh cilantro

1½ tablespoons Sriracha

2   teaspoons soy sauce

½   teaspoon dark (Asian) sesame oil

1   jalapeño pepper, seeded and minced

1 Heat canola oil in Dutch oven over medium-high heat. Add half of turkey and cook, stirring often, until no longer pink, about 3 minutes. Transfer to plate. Repeat with remaining turkey. Add garlic to Dutch oven and cook, stirring constantly, until fragrant, 30 seconds.

2 Add broth and water and bring to boil. Add noodles and return to boil. Reduce heat and simmer until tender, about 3 minutes. Return turkey to pan and cook just until heated through, about 1 minute.

3 Remove pan from heat and stir in bok choy, 2 scallions, ¼ cup cilantro, Sriracha, soy sauce, and sesame oil. Ladle evenly into 4 bowls and top with remaining scallion, remaining ¼ cup cilantro, and jalapeño.

4 **SmartPoints value per serving** (2 cups): 254 Cal, 5 g Total Fat, 1 g Sat Fat, 1,084 mg Sod, 26 g Total Carb, 3 g Sugar, 1 g Fib, 29 g Prot.

Eat better
Turkey breast can become tough and dry if it's overcooked. That's why in this recipe it's browned and removed from the Dutch oven, then added back to the soup to reheat just before serving.

Smoky turkey gumbo

serves 4   gluten free

- **2   teaspoons canola oil**
- **3   (5-ounce) turkey breast cutlets, cut into 1-inch chunks**
- **1¼ teaspoons Cajun spice**
- **1   onion, chopped**
- **1   celery stalk, thinly sliced**
- **1   green bell pepper, chopped**
- **2   garlic cloves, minced**
- **½   teaspoon smoked sweet paprika**
- **1   cup chicken broth**
- **1   (14½-ounce) can diced tomatoes**
- **1   fresh thyme sprig**
- **¼   teaspoon salt**
- **3   tablespoons chopped fresh flat-leaf parsley**

1 Heat 1 teaspoon oil in Dutch oven over medium-high heat. Sprinkle turkey with Cajun spice. Add half of turkey and cook, stirring often, until browned, about 5 minutes. Transfer to plate. Repeat with remaining turkey.

2 Add remaining 1 teaspoon oil to Dutch oven. Add onion, celery, and bell pepper and cook, stirring often, until vegetables are softened, 5 minutes. Add garlic and paprika and cook, stirring constantly, until fragrant, 30 seconds.

3 Stir in broth, tomatoes, and thyme sprig and bring to boil. Reduce heat and simmer until slightly thickened, about 8 minutes. Stir in turkey and salt and cook just until heated through, about 1 minute. Remove from heat and stir in parsley. Remove and discard thyme sprig.

1 **SmartPoints value per serving** (scant 1¼ cups): 191 Cal, 5 g Total Fat, 1 g Sat Fat, 876 mg Sod, 9 g Total Carb, 5 g Sugar, 2 g Fib, 28 g Prot.

Let's do this together
Do what Weight Watchers member Jane Freidinger does to curb impulse buys at the supermarket. She starts shopping from the back of the store—where you'll find zero Points foods like skinless boneless chicken breast and turkey cutlets—leaving less room in the cart for snack foods.

Gingery turkey noodle soup

serves 4

4   teaspoons olive oil

½   pound turkey breast cutlets, cut into ½-inch pieces

¼   teaspoon black pepper

2   leeks, halved lengthwise and thinly sliced, white and light green parts only

2   large carrots, thinly sliced

2   thin celery stalks, thinly sliced

2   garlic cloves, minced

2   teaspoons grated peeled fresh ginger

6   cups chicken broth

1½   cups wide egg noodles

2   tablespoons chopped fresh flat-leaf parsley

Salt, to taste

1 Heat 2 teaspoons oil in Dutch oven over medium-high heat. Sprinkle turkey with ⅛ teaspoon pepper. Add turkey and cook, stirring occasionally, just until cooked through, about 2 minutes. Transfer turkey to medium bowl and keep warm.

2 Heat remaining 2 teaspoons oil in same pot over medium heat. Add leeks, carrots, celery, and remaining ⅛ teaspoon pepper; cover and cook, stirring occasionally, until vegetables are tender, about 5 minutes. Add garlic and ginger; cook, stirring constantly, just until fragrant, about 30 seconds. Add broth, cover, and bring to boil over high heat.

3 Stir noodles into broth mixture; reduce heat and cook, covered, until noodles are tender, about 7 minutes. Stir in turkey and parsley and season to taste with salt.

4 **SmartPoints value per serving** (2 cups): 266 Cal, 9 g Total Fat, 2 g Sat Fat, 1,175 mg Sod, 23 g Total Carb, 5 g Sugar, 3 g Fib, 24 g Prot.

Eat better

Bulk up the veggies in this soup by adding 1 cup thawed frozen petite green peas along with the turkey and parsley in step 3.

**Gingery turkey
noodle soup**

Warm turkey salad with mint

serves 4   gluten free

People with weakened immune systems, like children, the elderly, and pregnant women, should avoid eating raw bean sprouts. You can substitute baby spinach or an Asian greens salad blend for the sprouts in this recipe.

¾   **pound turkey breast cutlets**

1   **teaspoon grated lime zest**

3   **tablespoons lime juice**

1   **tablespoon Asian fish sauce**

2   **teaspoons rice vinegar**

2   **teaspoons (Asian) dark sesame oil**

1   **teaspoon honey**

3   **cups bean sprouts**

2   **cups matchstick-cut carrots**

½   **English (seedless) cucumber, cut into matchstick-size strips**

1   **jalapeño pepper, halved lengthwise, seeded, and thinly sliced**

3   **tablespoons chopped fresh mint**

3   **tablespoons roasted unsalted cashews, chopped**

1½   **tablespoons sesame seeds, toasted**

1 Combine turkey and enough cold salted water to cover in large skillet; bring to boil. Reduce heat, cover and simmer until cooked through, about 5 minutes. Transfer to plate until cool enough to handle; shred.

2 Meanwhile, to make dressing, whisk together lime zest and juice, fish sauce, vinegar, oil, and honey in small bowl.

3 Toss together bean sprouts, carrots, cucumber, jalapeño, and 2 tablespoons mint in large bowl.

4 Divide salad evenly among 4 plates; top evenly with turkey. Drizzle with dressing and sprinkle with remaining 1 tablespoon mint, cashews, and sesame seeds.

3 **SmartPoints value per serving** (about 1 cup): 243 Cal, 9 g Total Fat, 1 g Sat Fat, 402 mg Sod, 18 g Total Carb, 8 g Sugar, 5 g Fib, 26 g Prot.

Penne with turkey, artichokes, and basil

serves 6

½   **pound penne**

4   **teaspoons olive oil**

1   **pound ground skinless turkey breast**

1   **red onion, finely chopped**

3   **garlic cloves, minced**

¾   **teaspoon salt**

¼   **teaspoon black pepper**

1   **(9-ounce) package frozen artichoke hearts, thawed**

½   **cup fresh basil leaves, chopped**

⅓   **cup grated pecorino or Parmesan**

1 Cook pasta according to package instructions, except cook 1 minute less than minimum time specified. Drain and reserve ¾ cup cooking liquid.

2 Meanwhile, heat 2 teaspoons oil in large skillet over medium-high heat. Add turkey, onion, half of garlic, ½ teaspoon salt, and ⅛ teaspoon pepper. Cook, breaking turkey apart with wooden spoon, until turkey is no longer pink, about 5 minutes. Transfer turkey to medium bowl.

3 Heat remaining 2 teaspoons oil in same skillet over medium heat. Add artichokes and remaining garlic. Cover and cook, stirring occasionally and breaking artichokes into pieces with side of spoon, until artichokes are tender, 5–6 minutes.

4 Add pasta and ½ cup cooking liquid to skillet. Stir in turkey, remaining ¼ teaspoon salt and remaining ⅛ teaspoon pepper. Cook, scraping up browned bits from bottom of pan, until pasta is al dente, about 2 minutes. (If pasta is dry, gradually add remaining ¼ cup cooking liquid.) Remove from heat and stir in basil and cheese.

6   **SmartPoints value per serving** (1⅓ cups): 298 Cal, 7 g Total Fat, 2 g Sat Fat, 442 mg Sod, 34 g Total Carb, 2 g Sugar, 3 g Fib, 25 g Prot.

Eat better

When you shop for ground turkey, read labels carefully. Only ground skinless turkey breast is zero Points on the WW Freestyle program. It's usually labeled 99% fat-free.

Turkey-basil stir-fry
with rice noodles

Turkey-basil stir-fry with rice noodles

serves 4

4   ounces thin rice noodles
¾   cup chicken broth
3   tablespoons soy sauce
1   tablespoon cornstarch
1   pound turkey breast cutlets, cut into thin strips
¼   teaspoon salt, or to taste
4   teaspoons canola oil
3   garlic cloves, finely chopped
4   teaspoons finely chopped peeled fresh ginger
¼   teaspoon red pepper flakes
4   cups small broccoli florets
2   small orange bell peppers, thinly sliced
4   scallions, cut into 1-inch pieces
¼   cup chopped fresh basil

1 Place noodles in large bowl; cover with boiling water. Let stand until noodles soften, about 3 minutes. Drain.

2 Meanwhile, whisk together broth, soy sauce, and cornstarch in small bowl until smooth. Set aside.

3 Sprinkle turkey with salt. Heat wok or large skillet over medium-high heat until drop of water sizzles in pan. Add 2 teaspoons oil and swirl to coat pan. Add turkey and stir-fry until browned and cooked through, about 4 minutes. Transfer to plate.

4 Wipe out wok and set over medium-high heat. Add remaining 2 teaspoons oil to wok. Add garlic, ginger, and red pepper flakes; stir-fry until fragrant, about 30 seconds. Add broccoli, bell pepper, and scallions; stir-fry until vegetables are crisp-tender, about 2 minutes. Add turkey and noodles to wok. Whisk broth mixture again and add to wok. Bring to boil; reduce heat and stir-fry until mixture thickens, about 1 minute. Remove from heat and stir in basil. Season to taste with additional salt, if desired.

5 **SmartPoints value per serving** (about 1¾ cups): 330 Cal, 8 g Total Fat, 1 g Sat Fat, 980 mg Sod, 34 g Total Carb, 3 g Sugar, 3 g Fib, 33 g Prot.

Eat better
Turkey breast cutlets are a delicious change from skinless boneless chicken breasts, but if you wish, you can use chicken breast instead of turkey in any of the recipes in this chapter.

Turkey bolognese with zucchini "noodles"

serves 4   **gluten free**

If you've got a vegetable spiralizer, use it to prepare the "noodles" instead of a vegetable peeler. The bolognese sauce freezes beautifully, so if you have time, make a double batch for an easy dinner later.

4	**teaspoons olive oil**
½	**pound ground skinless turkey breast**
½	**teaspoon salt**
1	**carrot, chopped**
1	**onion, chopped**
2	**garlic cloves, minced**
1	**(14½-ounce) can diced tomatoes**
1	**(9-ounce) package vacuum-packed cooked lentils**
⅓	**cup plus 2 tablespoons water**
1	**tablespoon sun-dried tomato paste or minced sun-dried tomatoes (not oil-packed)**
2	**tablespoons chopped fresh oregano, plus extra oregano leaves for garnish**
¼	**teaspoon plus ⅛ teaspoon black pepper**
3	**zucchini, cut into thin lengthwise ribbons using vegetable peeler**
4	**tablespoons grated Parmesan**

1 Heat 2 teaspoons oil in large skillet over medium-high heat. Add turkey and ¼ teaspoon salt and cook, stirring often, until no longer pink, about 3 minutes. Add 1 teaspoon oil, carrot, and onion and cook, stirring often, until carrot and onion are softened, about 5 minutes. Add garlic and cook, stirring constantly, until fragrant, 30 seconds.

2 Add tomatoes, lentils, ⅓ cup water, tomato paste, 2 tablespoons oregano, ⅛ teaspoon salt, and ¼ teaspoon pepper. Simmer, stirring occasionally, about 3 minutes, adding additional water if needed to prevent sticking.

3 Meanwhile, combine zucchini and remaining 2 tablespoons water in large microwavable bowl. Cover with wax paper and microwave on High until crisp-tender, about 2 minutes. Drain and transfer to large bowl. Add remaining 1 teaspoon oil, remaining ⅛ teaspoon salt, and remaining ⅛ teaspoon pepper; toss to coat.

4 Divide zucchini evenly among 4 plates; top evenly with sauce. Sprinkle evenly with Parmesan and garnish with oregano.

(3) **SmartPoints value per serving** (¾ cup zucchini, 1¼ cups sauce, and 1 tablespoon cheese): 284 Cal, 10 g Total Fat, 2 g Sat Fat, 630 mg Sod, 28 g Total Carb, 10 g Sugar, 9 g Fib, 24 g Prot.

Turkey bolognese with zucchini "noodles"

Turkey picadillo

serves 4   gluten free

1   tablespoon olive oil

1   small red onion, chopped

1   orange bell pepper, diced

2   large garlic cloves, minced

1   pound ground skinless
     turkey breast

1   teaspoon ground cumin

1   teaspoon dried oregano

¾   teaspoon salt

¼   teaspoon black pepper

1   (14½-ounce) can diced tomatoes

12   green olives, pitted and chopped

¼   cup raisins, coarsely chopped

¼   cup chicken broth

2   tablespoons balsamic vinegar

4   teaspoons tomato paste

1   Heat oil in large skillet over medium-high heat. Add onion and bell pepper; cook, stirring occasionally, until crisp-tender, about 3 minutes. Add garlic and cook, stirring constantly, just until fragrant, about 30 seconds.

2   Add turkey, cumin, oregano, salt, and pepper; cook, breaking turkey apart with wooden spoon, until turkey is no longer pink, about 5 minutes.

3   Stir in tomatoes, olives, raisins, broth, 1½ tablespoons vinegar, and tomato paste. Reduce heat and simmer, covered, until flavors are blended, about 5 minutes. Stir in remaining ½ tablespoon vinegar.

(4) SmartPoints value per serving (about 1¼ cups): 253 Cal, 7 g Total Fat, 1 g Sat Fat, 890 mg Sod, 19 g Total Carb, 12 g Sugar, 3 g Fib, 30 g Prot.

Turkey and broccoli with black bean sauce

serves 4

4	teaspoons canola oil
2	cups small broccoli florets
1	orange or yellow bell pepper, cut into 1-inch pieces
¾	pound ground skinless turkey breast
1	tablespoon minced peeled fresh ginger
2	garlic cloves, minced
3	scallions, thinly sliced
5	tablespoons water
3	tablespoons black bean sauce
1	tablespoon rice wine
1	tablespoon soy sauce
2	tablespoons coarsely chopped roasted unsalted peanuts

1 Heat 2 teaspoons oil in large skillet over medium-high heat. Add broccoli and pepper; cook, stirring constantly, until crisp-tender, about 2 minutes. Transfer to plate.

2 Heat remaining 2 teaspoons oil in same skillet. Add turkey, ginger, and garlic; cook, breaking turkey apart with wooden spoon, until turkey is no longer pink, about 3 minutes. Add scallions and cook, stirring often, until softened, 1 minute.

3 Reduce heat to medium. Stir in water, black bean sauce, rice wine, and soy sauce. Add broccoli and bell pepper to skillet and simmer until heated through, about 2 minutes.

4 Divide evenly among 4 shallow bowls and sprinkle with peanuts.

3 **SmartPoints value per serving** (1¼ cups stir-fry and ½ tablespoon peanuts): 215 Cal, 10 g Total Fat, 1 g Sat Fat, 559 mg Sod, 9 g Total Carb, 3 g Sugar, 2 g Fib, 24 g Prot.

Eat better
Ground skinless turkey breast is great for using in flavorful, saucy dishes like this one.

Sesame turkey stir-fry

Sesame turkey stir-fry

serves 4

2   teaspoons canola oil

1   red bell pepper, diced

1   carrot, diced

2   garlic cloves, minced

1   tablespoon minced peeled fresh ginger

1   pound ground skinless turkey breast

4   scallions, thinly sliced

1   cup thawed frozen green peas

2   tablespoons soy sauce

2   teaspoons (Asian) dark sesame oil

¼   teaspoon salt

⅛   teaspoon red pepper flakes

¼   cup chopped fresh cilantro

1⅓   cups hot cooked white rice

1   tablespoon sesame seeds, toasted

1 Heat canola oil in large skillet over medium-high heat. Add bell pepper and carrot and cook, stirring often, until softened, about 3 minutes. Add garlic and ginger and cook, stirring constantly, until fragrant, 30 seconds. Add turkey and cook, stirring often, until no longer pink, about 5 minutes. Add scallions and cook, stirring often, until scallions are softened, about 1 minute.

2 Stir in peas, soy sauce, sesame oil, salt, and pepper flakes and cook just until heated through, about 2 minutes. Remove from heat and stir in cilantro. Divide rice evenly among 4 bowls; top evenly with turkey mixture. Sprinkle with sesame seeds.

(4)   **SmartPoints value per serving** (1½ cups turkey stir-fry and ⅓ cup rice): 303 Cal, 8 g Total Fat, 1 g Sat Fat, 766 mg Sod, 26 g Total Carb, 4 g Sugar, 4 g Fib, 32 g Prot.

Turkey rigatoni with eggplant and feta

serves 4

3   cups rigatoni

1   (1-pound) eggplant, unpeeled, cut into ½-inch cubes

¾   teaspoon salt

⅛   teaspoon black pepper

3   teaspoons olive oil

½   pound ground skinless turkey breast

1   onion, chopped

1   garlic clove, crushed through a press

1   (14½-ounce) can diced tomatoes

3   tablespoons water

2   teaspoons tomato paste

¼   teaspoon red pepper flakes

⅓   cup crumbled reduced-fat feta

2   tablespoons chopped fresh flat-leaf parsley

1 Cook rigatoni according to package directions. Drain, reserving ¼ cup cooking liquid, and keep warm.

2 Meanwhile, preheat broiler. Line large baking sheet with foil; spray foil with nonstick spray.

3 Place eggplant on baking sheet; spray lightly with olive oil nonstick spray. Sprinkle with ¼ teaspoon salt and pepper and toss to coat. Spread to form even layer. Broil 5 inches from heat until tender and well browned, stirring once, about 10 minutes.

4 Meanwhile, heat 2 teaspoons oil in large skillet over medium-high heat. Add turkey and ¼ teaspoon salt and cook, stirring often, until no longer pink, about 3 minutes. Add remaining 1 teaspoon oil and onion and cook, stirring often, until softened, about 5 minutes. Add garlic and cook, stirring constantly, until fragrant, 30 seconds.

5 Add tomatoes, water, tomato paste, remaining ¼ teaspoon salt, and pepper flakes and bring to boil. Reduce heat and simmer, 2 minutes. Stir in eggplant, pasta, and cooking liquid, and cook just until heated through, about 2 minutes.

6 Divide evenly among 4 bowls and sprinkle evenly with feta and parsley.

8 **SmartPoints value per serving** (1¾ cups): 388 Cal, 7 g Total Fat, 2 g Sat Fat, 798 mg Sod, 57 g Total Carb, 8 g Sugar, 6 g Fib, 25 g Prot.

Let's do this together

Weight Watchers member René Falgout saves time grocery shopping by doing it at 6:30 on Saturday mornings. Then she's stocked up to cook meals on the weekend for the entire week—even the lunches she packs for work. She not only saves time, she sets herself up to resist fast food on time-crunched weeknights.

Turkey tacos in lettuce wraps

serves 4   gluten free   under 20 minutes

Taco filling

4   teaspoons canola oil

1   pound ground skinless
        turkey breast

1   small red onion, finely chopped

1   tablespoon Mexican seasoning
        blend or taco seasoning blend

⅛   teaspoon salt

1   large garlic clove, minced

1   yellow or orange bell pepper,
        thinly sliced

8   large romaine or Bibb
        lettuce leaves

Pico de gallo

1   large tomato, chopped

½   small onion, diced

2   tablespoons chopped
        fresh cilantro

½   jalapeño pepper, seeded
        and minced

1   tablespoon lime juice

⅛   teaspoon salt

1 To make filling, heat oil in large nonstick skillet over medium heat. Add turkey, onion, seasoning blend, and salt; cook, breaking up meat with side of spoon, until meat is no longer pink, about 5 minutes. Add garlic and cook, stirring constantly, just until fragrant, about 30 seconds. Add bell pepper and cook, stirring occasionally, until crisp-tender, about 1 minute.

2 Meanwhile, to make pico de gallo, stir together all ingredients in medium bowl.

3 Spoon turkey mixture evenly onto lettuce leaves and top evenly with pico de gallo.

1 **SmartPoints value per serving** (2 lettuce wraps): 189 Cal, 7 g Total Fat, 1 g Sat Fat, 1,100 mg Sod, 8 g Total Carb, 4 g Sugar, 2 g Fib, 26 g Prot.

Five-spice turkey with mushrooms

serves 4

Pea shoots are immature pea plants. They're crunchy and taste like very mild green peas. If you can't find them, you can use watercress or baby spinach in this recipe. Cook them just a couple of minutes until slightly wilted, maintaining their crisp texture.

4	**teaspoons canola oil**
1	**onion, thinly sliced**
2	**garlic cloves, crushed through a press**
1	**pound ground skinless turkey breast**
½	**teaspoon Chinese five-spice powder**
½	**teaspoon salt**
¼	**teaspoon black pepper**
½	**pound cremini mushrooms, quartered**
1	**zucchini, halved lengthwise and sliced**
1½	**cups lightly packed fresh pea shoots or watercress**
⅓	**cup water**
2	**tablespoons soy sauce**
¼	**cup chopped fresh cilantro**

1 Heat 2 teaspoons oil in large skillet over medium-high heat. Add onion and cook, stirring occasionally, until softened, about 3 minutes. Add garlic and cook, stirring constantly, until fragrant, about 30 seconds. Add turkey, five-spice powder, salt, and pepper. Cook, breaking turkey apart with wooden spoon, until turkey is no longer pink, about 5 minutes. Transfer turkey to medium bowl.

2 Heat remaining 2 teaspoons oil in same skillet. Add mushrooms and cook, stirring often, until tender, about 4 minutes. Add zucchini slices and cook, stirring constantly, until just crisp-tender, about 2 minutes. Stir in turkey mixture, pea shoots, water, and soy sauce; cook, stirring constantly, just until pea shoots are wilted, about 2 minutes.

3 Divide evenly among 4 shallow bowls; sprinkle with cilantro.

1 **SmartPoints value per serving** (1¼ cups): 212 Cal, 7 g Total Fat, 1 g Sat Fat, 792 mg Sod, 8 g Total Carb, 4 g Sugar, 2 g Fib, 31 g Prot.

Five-spice turkey with mushrooms

Green chile
and Cheddar
turkey burgers

Green chile and Cheddar turkey burgers

serves 4

1 **pound ground skinless turkey breast**

1 **small zucchini, shredded**

⅓ **cup plain dried bread crumbs**

1 **teaspoon chili powder**

½ **teaspoon ground cumin**

½ **teaspoon salt**

2 **teaspoons canola oil**

1 **(4-ounce) can diced fire-roasted green chiles, drained**

⅓ **cup shredded reduced-fat sharp Cheddar**

½ **small red onion, thinly sliced**

1 **tomato, sliced**

4 **whole wheat sandwich thins, toasted**

1 Combine turkey, zucchini, bread crumbs, chili powder, cumin, and salt in large bowl. Shape into 4 (¾-inch-thick) patties.

2 Heat oil in large nonstick skillet over medium heat. Add patties and cook until browned and instant-read thermometer inserted into sides of patties registers 165°F, about 6 minutes per side.

3 Meanwhile, stir together chiles and Cheddar in medium bowl.

4 Top burgers evenly with chile mixture. Reduce heat to low; cover skillet and cook until cheese melts, about 2 minutes. Serve burgers, onion, and tomato in sandwich thins.

6 **SmartPoints value per serving** (1 burger): 321 Cal, 8 g Total Fat, 2 g Sat Fat, 954 mg Sod, 32 g Total Carb, 6 g Sugar, 7 g Fib, 33 g Prot.

Turkish turkey pita pizzas

serves 4

2	teaspoons canola oil
¾	pound ground skinless turkey breast
1	small red onion, halved and sliced
3	large garlic cloves, minced
1¼	teaspoons ground cumin
1	teaspoon paprika
½	teaspoon salt
¼	teaspoon ground allspice
¼	teaspoon cinnamon
1	(8-ounce) can tomato sauce
4	(7-inch) whole wheat pocketless pita breads
1	large tomato, diced
1	cup whole cilantro leaves

1 Preheat oven to 475°F; spray 2 baking sheets with nonstick spray.

2 Heat oil in large nonstick skillet over medium heat. Add turkey and onion and cook, breaking up turkey with wooden spoon, until turkey is no longer pink and onion is softened, about 6 minutes. Add garlic, cumin, paprika, salt, allspice, and cinnamon; cook, stirring constantly, until fragrant, 1 minute. Stir in tomato sauce and cook, stirring occasionally, 2 minutes.

3 Place pitas on baking sheets and top each evenly with turkey mixture (scant ¾ cup for each pita). Bake until undersides of pitas are crisp, about 8 minutes. Top evenly with tomato and cilantro.

3 **SmartPoints value per serving** (1 pizza): 219 Cal, 5 g Total Fat, 1 g Sat Fat, 886 mg Sod, 24 g Total Carb, 4 g Sugar, 4 g Fib, 23 g Prot.

Turkish turkey
pita pizzas

Turkey posole with radish-scallion topping

serves 4   gluten free

2	teaspoons canola oil
1	pound ground skinless turkey breast
1	onion, chopped
2	garlic cloves, minced
3	cups reduced-sodium chicken broth
1	(15-ounce) can hominy, rinsed and drained
1	(14½-ounce) can Mexican-style tomatoes
1	tablespoon chopped chipotle en adobo
2	teaspoons dried oregano
1	teaspoon salt
¼	cup shredded reduced-fat Cheddar
4	radishes, finely chopped
3	scallions, thinly sliced on diagonal

1 Heat oil in Dutch oven over medium-high heat. Add turkey and onion and cook, breaking turkey up with wooden spoon, until browned, about 6 minutes. Add garlic and cook, stirring constantly, until fragrant, 30 seconds.

2 Stir in broth, hominy, tomatoes, chipotle en adobo, oregano, and salt; bring to boil. Reduce heat and simmer, uncovered, stirring posole occasionally, until slightly thickened, about 10 minutes.

3 Ladle posole evenly into bowls and top with Cheddar, radishes, and scallions.

② **SmartPoints value per serving** (1¾ cups posole and 1 tablespoon cheese): 284 Cal, 7 g Total Fat, 2 g Sat Fat, 1,093 mg Sod, 25 g Total Carb, 5 g Sugar, 5 g Fib, 32 g Prot.

Turkey kafta salad

serves 4

1	**pound ground skinless turkey breast**
½	**cup chopped fresh parsley**
2	**tablespoons chopped fresh mint**
¼	**small onion, finely chopped**
2	**garlic cloves, minced**
1	**teaspoon ground cumin**
1	**teaspoon ground coriander**
¼	**teaspoon cinnamon**
¼	**teaspoon cayenne**
¼	**teaspoon salt**
½	**teaspoon coarsely ground black pepper**
2	**teaspoons canola oil**
5	**ounces baby spinach**
2	**tomatoes, cut into thin wedges**
1	**English (seedless) cucumber, peeled and sliced**

Tahini dressing

3	**tablespoons tahini**
3	**tablespoons hot water**
2	**tablespoons lemon juice**
1	**garlic clove, minced**
⅛	**teaspoon salt**
⅛	**teaspoon black pepper**

1 Combine turkey, parsley, mint, onion, garlic, cumin, coriander, cinnamon, cayenne, salt, and pepper in large bowl. Shape into 8 patties.

2 Heat oil in large nonstick skillet over medium heat. Add patties to skillet and cook, turning occasionally, until instant-read thermometer inserted into sides of patties registers 165°F, about 8 minutes.

3 Meanwhile, to make dressing, whisk together all ingredients in small bowl until smooth, adding additional water a few drops at a time if needed for desired consistency.

4 Divide spinach, tomato, and cucumber evenly among 4 plates. Top each with 2 kafta patties and drizzle with dressing.

3 **SmartPoints value per serving** (about 2 cups salad, 2 kaftas, and 2 tablespoons dressing): 268 Cal, 11 g Total Fat, 2 g Sat Fat, 319 mg Sod, 11 g Total Carb, 4 g Sugar, 4 g Fib, 32 g Prot.

Sweet and spicy salmon with Asian broccoli salad

serves 4   under 20 minutes

Salmon plays the perfect host to the sweet-and-sour flavors that make up much of Asian cooking. We opt for wild salmon from Alaska, either sockeye or king, as they bring richer flavors as well as a healthier ecology to the table than their farm-raised counterparts. In this recipe, broccoli slaw and cilantro provide a fresh, green, and crunchy balance to the fatty, rich salmon that has been quickly seared and seasoned with five-spice powder. A week-day special that is ready in 20 minutes, it could pass for dinner-party fare.

1   tablespoon packed light brown sugar

1   teaspoon five-spice powder

¼   teaspoon salt

4   (¼-pound) pieces skinless wild salmon fillet

2   tablespoons soy sauce

2   tablespoons rice vinegar

2   teaspoons Asian (dark) sesame oil

1   (12-ounce) package broccoli slaw

¼   cup chopped fresh cilantro

3   scallions, thinly sliced

1 Preheat broiler. Spray broiler pan with nonstick spray and place about 6 inches from heat until very hot.

2 Stir together brown sugar, five-spice powder, and salt in small bowl. Sprinkle mixture over tops of salmon fillets. Carefully place salmon fillets on hot broiler pan and broil until browned on outside and opaque in center, about 7 minutes.

3 Meanwhile, whisk together soy sauce, vinegar, and oil in large bowl. Add broccoli slaw, cilantro, and scallions and toss to combine. Serve slaw with salmon.

2 **SmartPoints value per serving** (1 salmon fillet and 1 cup slaw): 230 Cal, 10 g Total Fat, 1 g Sat Fat, 659 mg Sod, 10 g Total Carb, 5 g Sugar, 3 g Fib, 25 g Prot.

Grilled salmon with pea and corn salad

serves 6   gluten free

This recipe is all freshness and sunshine. Just thinking about it cheers us up! We start by cooking peas and corn until they're crisp-tender, then add tomatoes, scallions, radishes, and basil for more color and texture. This is a good moment to experiment: Heirloom tomatoes, such as Pink Brandywine or Golden Globes, are wonderful choices. To keep the salmon moist and silky, be careful not to overcook it. The USDA recommends an internal temperature of 145°F, measured at the thickest part of the fish.

1	**(10-ounce) box frozen baby peas**
1	**(10-ounce) box frozen corn kernels**
3	**large plum tomatoes, diced**
3	**scallions, thinly sliced**
6	**radishes, thinly sliced**
¼	**cup thinly sliced fresh basil**
1	**tablespoon extra-virgin olive oil**
1	**tablespoon sherry vinegar or cider vinegar**
1	**teaspoon salt**
½	**teaspoon black pepper**
6	**(5-ounce) skin-on salmon fillets**
	Lemon wedges

1 To make salad, bring large pot of lightly salted water to boil. Add peas and corn and cook just until crisp-tender, about 2 minutes. Drain in colander, then hold under cold running water to stop cooking; drain again.

2 Stir together peas and corn, tomatoes, scallions, radishes, basil, oil, vinegar, ½ teaspoon salt, and ¼ teaspoon pepper in serving bowl.

3 Meanwhile, spray large ridged grill pan with nonstick spray and set over medium heat.

4 Sprinkle flesh side of salmon with remaining ½ teaspoon salt and remaining ¼ teaspoon pepper. Place fillets in pan skin side up, and cook until just opaque in center, turning once, about 4 minutes per side. Serve salmon with salad and lemon wedges. Remove salmon skin before eating.

1 **SmartPoints value per serving** (1 salmon fillet and about 1 cup salad): 265 Cal, 10 g Total Fat, 2 g Sat Fat, 495 mg Sod, 18 g Total Carb, 5 g Sugar, 4 g Fib, 27 g Prot.

Eat better
Make salmon part of your regular dinner routine. It's one of the best sources of heart-healthy omega-3 fatty acids, tastes incredibly delicious, and cooks in less than 10 minutes.

Salmon burgers with
cucumber salsa

Salmon burgers with cucumber salsa

serves 4

We love burgers, especially when we swap in a zero Points food like salmon for the beef and mix in mustard and fresh cilantro for a kick of flavor. The salsa is a snap to make: Combine English cucumbers, lime juice, and jalapeño pepper sauce. We use toasted multigrain English muffins for the bun. All in all, a taste sensation.

1   **pound skinless salmon fillet, finely diced**

1   **small shallot, finely chopped**

2   **tablespoons chopped fresh cilantro**

½   **teaspoon Dijon mustard**

¼   **teaspoon black pepper**

¼   **teaspoon salt**

1   **cup diced English (seedless) cucumber**

Juice of ½ lime

¼   **teaspoon jalapeño pepper sauce**

1   **cup watercress leaves**

4   **multigrain English muffins, split and toasted**

Lemon wedges

1   Combine salmon, shallot, 1 tablespoon cilantro, mustard, pepper, and ⅛ teaspoon salt in medium bowl; mix to combine. Form into 4 patties, each about ½-inch thick. Spray large skillet with nonstick spray and set over medium heat. Add patties and cook until lightly browned and cooked through, 5–6 minutes per side.

2   Meanwhile, to make salsa, combine cucumber, lime juice, pepper sauce, remaining 1 tablespoon cilantro, and remaining ⅛ teaspoon salt in medium bowl.

3   Layer ¼ cup watercress, 1 burger, and ⅓ cup salsa into each English muffin. Serve with lemon wedges.

4   **SmartPoints value per serving** (1 burger): 329 Cal, 9 g Total Fat, 1 g Sat Fat, 420 mg Sod, 33 g Carb, 2 g Sugar, 2 g Fib, 29 g Prot.

Tandoori roasted salmon with vegetables

serves 4   gluten free

If you're looking for something rich and hearty, look no more. This delicious main course uses traditional Indian spices to flavor both the fish and the vegetables. It features garam masala, a spice blend that lends warmth to a dish and typically consists of cumin, cardamom, coriander, cinnamon, mace, cloves, nutmeg, and black peppercorns, though the mix of spices varies by region in India. Garam means "hot" and masala means "spice," but the heat in this recipe comes from the cayenne.

1   **teaspoon ground ginger**
1   **teaspoon garam masala**
1   **teaspoon ground coriander**
¼   **teaspoon cayenne**
¾   **teaspoon salt**
¼   **teaspoon sugar**
2   **pounds mixed zucchini and yellow squash, sliced**
1   **large shallot, thinly sliced**
2   **teaspoons olive oil**
4   **(5-ounce) skinless salmon fillets**
3   **tablespoons plain low-fat yogurt**
Lemon wedges

1 Place one rack in upper third of oven. Preheat oven to 500°F. Spray large rimmed baking sheet with nonstick spray.

2 Stir together ginger, garam masala, coriander, cayenne, salt, and sugar in small bowl.

3 Place zucchini and squash and shallot on baking sheet. Drizzle with oil and 2 teaspoons spice mixture and toss to coat. Spread in even layer toward outer edge of pan. Place salmon in center of pan.

4 Add yogurt to remaining spice mixture in bowl; spoon over salmon. Bake in upper third of oven until fish is just opaque, 12–14 minutes. Serve with lemon wedges.

1 **SmartPoints value per serving** (1 salmon fillet and 1 cup vegetables): 372 Cal, 22 g Total Fat, 5 g Sat Fat, 540 mg Sod, 12 g Total Carb, 9 g Sugar, 3 g Fib, 32 g Prot.

Tandoori roasted
salmon with vegetables

Tuna with caramelized onions and fennel

serves 4   gluten free

Tuna is often relegated to the sushi counter, but there is simply no reason to do so. Slowly cooked (some might say candied) red onions and fennel are the perfect complement to the richness of tuna. Red-wine vinegar (sherry vinegar would work, too) adds a hint of acid and brightens the dish.

1   **tablespoon olive oil**

2   **red onions, thinly sliced**

1   **fennel bulb, thinly sliced**

½   **teaspoon salt**

⅛   **teaspoon ground black pepper**

1   **tablespoon red-wine vinegar**

2   **teaspoons chopped fresh rosemary**

4   **(5-ounce) tuna steaks (about ¾-inch thick)**

¼   **teaspoon cracked black pepper**

Lemon wedges

1 Heat oil in large skillet over medium heat. Add onions, fennel, ¼ teaspoon salt, and ground black pepper; cover and cook, stirring occasionally, until onions are browned and very soft, about 14 minutes. Stir in vinegar and rosemary. Transfer onion mixture to small bowl; cover and keep warm.

2 Sprinkle tuna with remaining ¼ teaspoon salt and cracked pepper. Spray same skillet with olive oil nonstick spray and set over medium-high heat. Add tuna and cook until lightly browned and barely pink in center, about 3 minutes per side. Transfer steaks to plates; top evenly with onion mixture.

1 **SmartPoints value per serving** (1 tuna steak and ½ cup onion mixture): 224 Cal, 5 g Total Fat, 1 g Sat Fat, 376 mg Sod, 10 g Total Carb, 2 g Sugar, 3 g Fib, 35 g Prot.

Sautéed tilapia with almonds and cherries

serves 4   gluten free   under 20 minutes

1   tablespoon sliced almonds

3   teaspoons extra-virgin olive oil

4   (5-ounce) tilapia, flounder,
    or sole fillets

¼   teaspoon salt

¼   teaspoon black pepper

1   small onion, chopped

2   tablespoons dry vermouth,
    dry white wine, or chicken broth

½   cup pitted fresh sweet
    cherries, halved

⅓   cup vegetable broth

½   teaspoon dried thyme

1   Place almonds in small skillet; cook over medium-low heat, stirring constantly, until lightly toasted and fragrant, about 4 minutes. Transfer to bowl.

2   Heat 2 teaspoons oil in large nonstick skillet over medium heat. Sprinkle fish with salt and pepper. Add fish to skillet and cook until just opaque in center, about 2 minutes on each side. Transfer to plate and keep warm.

3   Heat remaining 1 teaspoon oil in same skillet. Add onion and cook, stirring frequently, until softened, about 2 minutes. Add vermouth; bring to boil, stirring constantly to scrape browned bits from bottom of skillet. Add cherries, vegetable broth, and thyme; bring to boil. Cook until most of liquid evaporates, about 1 minute. Top fish with cherry mixture and sprinkle with almonds.

2 **SmartPoints value per serving** (1 tilapia fillet, ¼ cup cherry mixture, and ¾ teaspoon almonds): 179 Cal, 5 g Total Fat, 1 g Sat Fat, 252 mg Sod, 5 g Total Carb, 3 g Sugar, 1 g Fib, 27 g Prot.

Grilled tuna with
cucumber-noodle salad

Grilled tuna with cucumber-noodle salad

serves 4   gluten free

3   tablespoons lime juice

2   tablespoons rice vinegar

1½   tablespoons sugar

1   teaspoon chili-garlic sauce

½   teaspoon salt

⅓   cup hot water

½   (8-ounce) package thin
      rice noodles

6   radishes, thinly sliced

½   English (seedless) cucumber,
      halved lengthwise, seeded,
      and sliced

¼   red onion, thinly sliced

¼   cup loosely packed fresh cilantro
      leaves, plus additional for garnish

4   (5-ounce) tuna steaks

1   teaspoon olive oil

½   teaspoon black pepper

Lime wedges

1 Combine lime juice, vinegar, sugar, chili-garlic sauce, and ¼ teaspoon salt in medium bowl. Add hot water and stir until sugar dissolves. Set aside to cool.

2 Meanwhile, cook rice noodles according to package directions. Rinse with cold water and drain. Add to lime juice mixture. Add radishes, cucumber, onion, and cilantro and toss to combine.

3 Heat ridged grill pan over medium-high heat. Brush tuna on all sides with oil. Sprinkle with remaining ¼ teaspoon salt and pepper. Place in pan and cook, turning once, 6 minutes for rare, or to desired doneness. Cut steaks across grain into ¼-inch-thick slices. Divide noodle salad among 4 plates. Top evenly with tuna and garnish with cilantro leaves. Serve with lime wedges.

5 **SmartPoints value per serving** (1 tuna steak and 1¼ cups noodle salad): 300 Cal, 3 g Total Fat, 1 g Sat Fat, 399 mg Sod, 32 g Total Carb, 6 g Sugar, 2 g Fib, 35 g Prot.

Swordfish and tomatoes with basil sauce

serves 4   gluten free

4   plum or other small
     tomatoes, halved

1   cup whole cherry tomatoes

1½   cups lightly packed fresh
     basil leaves

3   tablespoons chicken broth

3   tablespoons grated Parmesan

1   tablespoon chopped walnuts

1   garlic clove, chopped

2   teaspoons lemon juice

3   teaspoons olive oil

½   teaspoon salt

½   teaspoon black pepper

4   (5-ounce) swordfish steaks

1 Spray broiler rack with nonstick spray; preheat broiler.

2 Place all tomatoes on broiler rack and lightly spray with olive oil nonstick spray. Broil 5 inches from heat until tomatoes are softened, about 8 minutes.

3 Meanwhile, to make sauce, combine basil, broth, Parmesan, walnuts, garlic, lemon juice, 1 teaspoon oil, ¼ teaspoon salt, and ¼ teaspoon pepper in blender or food processor, and pulse until finely chopped. Set aside.

4 Heat remaining 2 teaspoons oil in large skillet over medium-high heat. Sprinkle fish with remaining ¼ teaspoon salt and remaining ¼ teaspoon pepper. Add fish to skillet and cook, turning once, until fish flakes easily with a fork, about 8 minutes.

5 Divide swordfish and tomatoes evenly among 4 plates and drizzle evenly with sauce.

2 **SmartPoints value per serving** (1 swordfish steak, 2 plum tomato halves, 2 cherry tomatoes, and 1 tablespoon sauce): 292 Cal, 16 g Total Fat, 4 g Sat Fat, 531 mg Sod, 6 g Total Carb, 3 g Sugar, 2 g Fib, 31 g Prot.

Swordfish and tomatoes with basil sauce

Arctic char with
watercress salad

Arctic char with watercress salad

serves 4   gluten free   under 20 minutes

4   (6-ounce) skin-on Arctic
    char fillets

¼   teaspoon plus ⅛ teaspoon salt

¼   teaspoon black pepper

½   cup chopped fresh mint

4   teaspoons Dijon mustard

1½   teaspoons honey

1   teaspoon prepared horseradish

1   teaspoon water

1   tablespoon sherry vinegar

1½   teaspoons olive oil

1   (4-ounce) bag watercress

2   mini-cucumbers, thinly sliced

½   small red onion, thinly sliced

1 Spray ridged grill pan with nonstick spray; set over medium heat until hot. Sprinkle flesh side of Arctic char with ¼ teaspoon salt and ⅛ teaspoon pepper. Place in grill pan and cook until lightly browned and just opaque in center, 4–5 minutes on each side.

2 Meanwhile, to make sauce, stir together mint, mustard, honey, horseradish, and water in small bowl. Set aside.

3 To make salad, whisk together vinegar, oil, remaining ⅛ teaspoon salt and remaining ⅛ teaspoon pepper in large bowl. Add watercress, cucumbers, and onion and toss to coat.

4 Remove skin from Arctic char and discard. Divide watercress salad evenly among 4 plates and top with Arctic char. Drizzle Arctic char evenly with sauce.

1 **SmartPoints value per serving** (1 Arctic char fillet, 1¼ cups salad, and 2 teaspoons sauce): 327 Cal, 15 g Total Fat, 0 g Sat Fat, 405 mg Sod, 7 g Total Carb, 4 g Sugar, 2 g Fib, 30 g Prot.

Eat better
Arctic char is a member of the trout and salmon family. It's a great choice since it is farmed in an ecologically responsible manner.

Tilapia and asparagus with spicy marinara

serves 4   gluten free

1   pound asparagus, trimmed
½   teaspoon black pepper
¼   teaspoon salt
4   (5-ounce) tilapia fillets
2   cups good-quality marinara sauce
2   anchovy fillets, chopped
⅛   teaspoon red pepper flakes

1 Spray broiler rack with nonstick spray; preheat broiler.

2 Place asparagus on broiler rack. Spray lightly with olive oil nonstick spray and sprinkle with ¼ teaspoon black pepper and ⅛ teaspoon salt; toss to coat. Broil 5 inches from heat, turning once, until crisp-tender, 8 minutes. Transfer asparagus to plate and cover to keep warm.

3 Sprinkle tilapia with remaining ¼ teaspoon black pepper and remaining ⅛ teaspoon salt; place on same broiler rack. Broil until fish is just opaque in center, about 8 minutes.

4 Meanwhile, combine marinara, anchovies, and pepper flakes in medium saucepan. Heat over medium heat until just simmering, about 3 minutes. Divide tilapia and asparagus evenly among 4 plates; spoon sauce evenly over tilapia.

3 **SmartPoints value per serving** (1 tilapia fillet, about 5 asparagus spears, and ½ cup sauce): 210 Cal, 4 g Total Fat, 1 g Sat Fat, 824 mg Sod, 15 g Total Carb, 9 g Sugar, 5 g Fib, 31 g Prot.

Salmon and Kalamata olive sandwiches

serves 4   no cook   under 20 minutes

1   (7½-ounce) can water-packed salmon, drained and flaked

½   cup peeled, seeded, and chopped cucumber

¼   cup chopped red onion

8   Kalamata olives, pitted and chopped

3   tablespoons plain fat-free Greek yogurt

2   tablespoons chopped fresh mint

Grated zest and juice of ½ lime

Few drops hot pepper sauce

4   (6-inch) whole wheat pita breads, halved

4   red leaf lettuce leaves, halved

2   plum tomatoes, sliced

1 Stir together salmon, cucumber, onion, olives, yogurt, mint, lime zest and juice, and pepper sauce in medium bowl.

2 Fill pita halves evenly with lettuce, salmon salad, and tomatoes.

2 **SmartPoints value per serving** (2 filled pita halves): 178 Cal, 4 g Total Fat, 1 g Sat Fat, 439 mg Sod, 20 g Total Carb, 2 g Sugar, 4 g Fib, 15 g Prot.

Eat better

If you'd like, you can serve the salmon salad on top of arugula, baby kale, or spinach instead of turning it into a sandwich.

Cornmeal spice-crusted tilapia

serves 4   gluten free   under 20 minutes

2   **tablespoons cornmeal**
2   **teaspoons smoked sweet paprika**
1   **teaspoon Old Bay seasoning**
1   **teaspoon black pepper**
1   **teaspoon packed brown sugar**
1   **teaspoon dried thyme**
4   **(5-ounce) tilapia fillets**
4   **teaspoons canola oil**
Lemon wedges

1 On large sheet of wax paper, mix together cornmeal, paprika, Old Bay seasoning, black pepper, brown sugar, and thyme. Coat fish fillets in spice mixture, pressing so it adheres.

2 Heat large heavy skillet over medium-high heat; add oil. Add fish and spray with nonstick spray. Cook until deeply browned and just opaque in center, about 4 minutes per side. Serve with lemon wedges.

2 **SmartPoints value per serving** (1 tilapia fillet): 180 Cal, 6 g Total Fat, 1 g Sat Fat, 213 mg Sod, 5 g Total Carb, 1 g Sugar, 1 g Fib, 27 g Prot.

Eat better
Before you refrigerate fish, rinse it under cold running water and pat it dry. This simple step cuts down on the bacteria on the fish's surface and slows spoilage. Always cook or freeze fish within a day or two after buying.

Cornmeal spice–crusted
tilapia served with
green bean and
tomato sauté, page 199

California
fish tacos

California fish tacos

serves 4   gluten free   under 20 minutes

1   **tablespoon lime juice**

2   **teaspoons olive oil**

¾   **teaspoon chili powder**

¾   **teaspoon ground coriander**

½   **teaspoon salt**

3   **(¼-pound) skinless red snapper fillets**

2   **cups thinly sliced green cabbage**

2   **scallions, thinly sliced**

½   **cup finely chopped red onion**

⅓   **cup coarsely chopped fresh cilantro**

1   **jalapeño pepper, seeded and minced**

8   **(6-inch) corn tortillas, warmed**

⅓   **cup light sour cream**

Lime wedges

1 Spray 7 x 11-inch baking dish with nonstick spray.

2 Stir together lime juice, oil, chili powder, coriander, and salt in cup. Place fish in baking dish in one layer and brush with lime juice mixture. Cover with wax paper and microwave on High until fish is just opaque in center, about 3 minutes. Cut fish into small pieces.

3 Meanwhile, toss together cabbage, scallions, red onion, cilantro, and jalapeño in medium bowl.

4 Fill tortillas evenly with fish and cabbage mixture; top with sour cream. Serve with lime wedges.

5 **SmartPoints value per serving** (2 tacos): 272 Cal, 7 g Total Fat, 2 g Sat Fat, 592 mg Sod, 32 g Total Carb, 4 g Sugar, 5 g Fib, 22 g Prot.

Let's do this together

Member Kylei Cucinella always keeps tortillas on hand to speed up weeknight meals. She's creative: "I can use them for tacos, fajitas, or quesadillas, turn them into a pizza crust, or cut them up to make my own chips."

Salmon panzanella with fresh basil

serves 4   no cook   under 20 minutes

1   **teaspoon grated lemon zest**

2   **tablespoons lemon juice**

1   **tablespoon red-wine vinegar**

2   **teaspoons olive oil**

½   **teaspoon salt**

¼   **teaspoon black pepper**

4   **cups cherry tomatoes, halved, or quartered if large**

1   **small English (seedless) cucumber, quartered lengthwise and sliced**

½   **cup drained water-packed roasted red peppers, coarsely chopped**

½   **small red onion, thinly sliced**

8   **Kalamata olives, pitted and chopped**

2   **(6-ounce) cans skinless boneless wild Alaska salmon, broken into chunks**

3   **ounces whole wheat ciabatta bread, cut into cubes and toasted**

1½   **cups fresh basil leaves, torn**

1   Whisk together lemon zest and juice, vinegar, oil, salt, and black pepper in large bowl. Stir in tomatoes, cucumber, red peppers, onion, and olives.

2   Add salmon and bread to bowl and toss gently to coat. Let stand until bread soaks up some of juices, about 5 minutes. Stir in basil and serve at once.

3   **SmartPoints value per serving** (2 cups): 374 Cal, 14 g Total Fat, 2 g Sat Fat, 918 mg Sod, 24 g Total Carb, 8 g Sugar, 4 g Fib, 39 g Prot.

Eat better

If you'd like to switch out the salmon for another zero Points ingredient, you can make this salad with a 15½-ounce can of chickpeas, rinsed and drained.

Salmon panzanella
with fresh basil

Tuna salad with mango and tomato

serves 4   gluten free   no cook   under 20 minutes

3   tablespoons reduced-fat
    mayonnaise

½   teaspoon grated lime zest

2   teaspoons lime juice

½   teaspoon salt

¼   teaspoon black pepper

2   (5-ounce) cans water-packed
    light tuna, drained and flaked

3   celery stalks, finely chopped

½   cup diced red onion

2   tablespoons chopped fresh mint

1   head Bibb lettuce, separated
    into leaves

2   mangoes, peeled, pitted,
    and sliced

2   tomatoes, cored and cut into
    thin wedges

¼   cup roasted unsalted cashews,
    finely chopped

1 Stir together mayonnaise, lime zest and juice, salt, and pepper in medium bowl. Add tuna, celery, onion, and mint and stir gently to combine.

2 Arrange lettuce leaves evenly on 4 plates. Top evenly with tuna salad; surround with mango and tomatoes. Sprinkle evenly with cashews.

3 **SmartPoints value per serving** (1 plate): 284 Cal, 9 g Total Fat, 2 g Sat Fat, 611 mg Sod, 35 g Total Carb, 27 g Sugar, 5 g Fib, 21 g Prot.

Tuna, bean, and olive salad

serves 4   gluten free   no cook   under 20 minutes

- **2** (5-ounce) cans water-packed solid white tuna, drained and flaked
- **1** (15½-ounce) can navy beans, rinsed and drained
- **1** red bell pepper, diced
- **1** small red onion, chopped
- **¼** cup pitted Kalamata olives, chopped
- **¼** cup chopped fresh flat-leaf parsley
- **1** tablespoon chopped fresh oregano or 1 teaspoon dried
- **1** garlic clove, minced
- **4** teaspoons extra-virgin olive oil
- **2** tablespoons balsamic vinegar
- **¼** teaspoon salt
- **¼** teaspoon black pepper
- **4** cups baby arugula

1 Combine tuna, beans, bell pepper, onion, olives, parsley, oregano, garlic, oil, vinegar, black pepper, and salt in large bowl. Toss gently to combine.

2 Divide arugula evenly among 4 plates and top with tuna mixture.

2 **SmartPoints value per serving** (1½ cups tuna salad and 1 cup arugula): 296 Cal, 9 g Total Fat, 2 g Sat Fat, 887 mg Sod, 29 g Total Carb, 3 g Sugar, 7 g Fib, 26 g Prot.

Eat better
To add more veggies to this salad, arrange halved cherry tomatoes and sliced cucumbers around each plate.

Shrimp and cherry tomatoes with feta

serves 4   gluten free   under 20 minutes

2   teaspoons olive oil

1¼   pounds medium peeled and
       deveined shrimp

¼   teaspoon salt

¼   teaspoon black pepper

1   pint cherry tomatoes, halved

2   garlic cloves, finely chopped

½   teaspoon dried oregano

¼   cup chicken broth

3   tablespoons crumbled feta

¼   cup chopped fresh dill

1 Heat oil in large skillet over medium-high heat. Sprinkle shrimp with salt and pepper; add to skillet and cook, stirring, until shrimp begin to turn pink, about 2 minutes.

2 Add tomatoes, garlic, and oregano and cook until tomatoes soften, about 1 minute. Add broth and cook, stirring to scrape up browned bits from bottom of pan, until shrimp are opaque in center, about 2 minutes. Stir in feta and cook 1 minute longer. Remove from heat and stir in dill. Serve immediately.

(2) **SmartPoints value per serving** (about ⅔ cup): 158 Cal, 5 g Total Fat, 2 g Sat Fat, 1,078 mg Sod, 5 g Total Carb, 2 g Sugar, 1 g Fib, 21 g Prot.

Eat better
Because this dish is made from mostly zero Points ingredients, we've stirred in some full-fat feta cheese to give a creamy texture and great flavor.

Corn, tomato, and shrimp sauté

serves 4   gluten free   under 20 minutes

2   teaspoons olive oil

1   pound medium peeled
     and deveined shrimp

½   cup chopped onion

2   garlic cloves, minced

1½   cups fresh corn kernels
     (from 2 ears)

1   pint cherry tomatoes

½   cup chopped fresh basil

1   tablespoon lemon juice

½   teaspoon salt

¼   teaspoon coarsely ground
     black pepper

1 Heat 1 teaspoon oil in large nonstick skillet over medium heat. Add shrimp and cook until lightly golden, about 1 minute on each side. Transfer shrimp to plate.

2 Heat remaining 1 teaspoon oil in skillet. Add onion and garlic; cook, stirring frequently, until onion starts to soften, about 1 minute. Stir in corn and cook until crisp-tender, about 1 minute. Add tomatoes and cook about 1 minute. Add shrimp and cook, stirring frequently, until heated through, 1–2 minutes. Remove skillet from heat and stir in basil, lemon juice, salt, and pepper.

1 **SmartPoints value per serving** (1 cup): 186 Cal, 4 g Total Fat, 1 g Sat Fat, 940 mg Sod, 21 g Total Carb, 5 g Sugar, 3 g Fib, 19 g Prot.

Shrimp and penne arrabiata

serves 4

Arrabiata means "angry" in Italian and is reflected by the generous amount of red pepper flakes in this classic Italian dish. Make it as "angry" as you like by adjusting the amount of pepper flakes.

6	**ounces penne**
1	**pound large peeled and deveined shrimp**
½	**teaspoon salt**
4	**teaspoons olive oil**
3	**large garlic cloves, minced**
¼	**teaspoon red pepper flakes**
1	**(14½-ounce) can fire-roasted diced tomatoes**
3	**tablespoons tomato paste**
3	**tablespoons chopped fresh basil**

1 Cook penne according to package directions. Drain and keep warm.

2 Meanwhile, sprinkle shrimp with ¼ teaspoon salt. Heat 2 teaspoons oil in large skillet over medium-high heat. Add half of shrimp and cook until just pink, about 2 minutes per side. Transfer to plate. Repeat with remaining shrimp.

3 Heat remaining 2 teaspoons oil in same skillet over medium heat. Add garlic and pepper flakes; cook, stirring constantly, until fragrant, about 30 seconds. Stir in tomatoes, tomato paste, and remaining ¼ teaspoon salt; cook until slightly thickened, about 3 minutes. Return shrimp to skillet along with pasta; cook, stirring, just until heated through, about 2 minutes longer.

4 Divide evenly among 4 plates and sprinkle with basil.

6 **SmartPoints value per serving** (1¾ cups): 326 Cal, 6 g Total Fat, 1 g Sat Fat, 671 mg Sod, 39 g Total Carb, 5 g Sugar, 3 g Fib, 30 g Prot.

Tex-Mex shrimp rolls

serves 4   no cook   under 20 minutes

½   **pound cooked medium peeled and deveined shrimp, halved or chopped**

3   **scallions, thinly sliced**

¼   **cup fat-free salsa**

¼   **cup reduced-fat mayonnaise**

3   **tablespoons fresh cilantro leaves**

¼   **teaspoon salt**

4   **light (reduced-calorie) whole wheat hot dog rolls, toasted**

Toss shrimp, scallions, salsa, mayonnaise, cilantro, and salt in medium bowl. Fill rolls evenly with shrimp mixture.

4 **SmartPoints value per serving** (1 filled roll): 209 Cal, 7 g Total Fat, 1 g Sat Fat, 1,039 mg Sod, 22 g Total Carb, 3 g Sugar, 4 g Fib, 17 g Prot.

Eat better
Line each roll with Bibb or leaf lettuce and thinly sliced plum tomatoes before adding the shrimp salad.

Asian shrimp and rice bowl

serves 4

1   cup quick-cooking brown rice

3   tablespoons rice vinegar

3   tablespoons ponzu sauce

2   teaspoons Asian (dark) sesame oil

1½   teaspoons grated peeled fresh ginger

1   teaspoon Sriracha (hot chili sauce)

1   pound cooked medium peeled and deveined shrimp

1   cucumber, peeled, halved lengthwise, seeded, and sliced

2   carrots, cut into matchstick strips

2   scallions, cut into matchstick strips

4   large radishes, cut into matchstick strips

1   cup bean sprouts

⅓   cup fresh whole cilantro leaves

1 Cook rice according to package directions (omit salt and butter if specified). Transfer to shallow bowl and let stand to cool 10 minutes.

2 Meanwhile, to make dressing, whisk together vinegar, ponzu sauce, oil, ginger, and Sriracha in small bowl.

3 Divide rice evenly among 4 shallow bowls. Top with shrimp, cucumber, carrots, scallions, radishes, and bean sprouts. Drizzle evenly with dressing and sprinkle with cilantro.

Note: People with weakened immune systems, like children, the elderly, and pregnant women, should avoid eating raw bean sprouts. You can omit them from this recipe if you wish.

4 **SmartPoints value per serving** (1 bowl): 278 Cal, 5 g Total Fat, 1 g Sat Fat, 1,350 mg Sod, 28 g Total Carb, 3 g Sugar, 3 g Fib, 29 g Prot.

Let's do this together

Member Anne Thalman doesn't mess around when it comes to saving time during the week. "We shop and cook all the meals—breakfast, lunch, and dinner—for the whole week over the weekend," she explains. "With two kids under four and both of us working full time, it's the only way to eat healthy, filling meals."

Asian shrimp
and rice bowl

Cajun shrimp with garlicky spinach grits

Cajun shrimp with garlicky spinach grits

serves 4   **gluten free**   **under 20 minutes**

Grits are coarse-ground corn that are cooked in water, broth, or milk and served for breakfast or as a side dish. They are a staple in the South and for good reason: They're quick to cook, can be served at any meal, and like rice or potatoes, take on the flavor of anything you add to them.

4	teaspoons olive oil
2	large garlic cloves, minced
1	(14½-ounce) can reduced-sodium chicken broth
¼	cup water
½	cup quick-cooking grits
3	cups firmly packed baby spinach
1¼	teaspoons Cajun or Creole seasoning
1	pound medium peeled and deveined shrimp
	Salt, to taste

1 Heat 2 teaspoons oil in large saucepan over medium heat. Add garlic and cook, stirring constantly, just until fragrant, 30 seconds. Add broth and water; bring to boil. Gradually stir in grits. Reduce heat and cook, covered, stirring occasionally, until grits thicken, about 5 minutes. Season to taste with salt.

2 Remove saucepan from heat and stir in spinach, in batches, until wilted. Cover and keep warm.

3 Meanwhile, stir together remaining 2 teaspoons oil and Cajun seasoning in medium bowl; add shrimp and toss to coat. Set large ridged grill pan over medium-high heat until hot. Add half of shrimp to pan and grill, turning once, until opaque in center, 3–4 minutes. Transfer to plate. Repeat with remaining shrimp. Season to taste with salt.

4 Divide grits mixture evenly among 4 shallow bowls; top evenly with shrimp.

(4) **SmartPoints value per serving** (½ cup grits mixture and about 8 shrimp): 209 Cal, 6 g Total Fat, 1 g Sat Fat, 1,127 mg Sod, 19 g Total Carb, 0 g Sugar, 1 g Fib, 19 g Prot.

Scallops with tomato-orange sauce

serves 4   gluten free

4   teaspoons olive oil

4   leeks, halved lengthwise and
    thinly sliced, white and light
    green parts only

1   (14½-ounce) can diced tomatoes

1   yellow bell pepper, thinly sliced

2   garlic cloves, minced

½   cup fresh orange juice

¼   teaspoon plus ⅛ teaspoon salt

3   tablespoons chopped fresh basil

1   pound sea scallops (about 16)

⅛   teaspoon black pepper

2   tablespoons black olive tapenade

1 To make sauce, heat 2 teaspoons oil in large nonstick skillet over medium-low heat. Add leeks; cover and cook, stirring occasionally, until softened, about 10 minutes. Stir in tomatoes, bell pepper, garlic, orange juice, and ¼ teaspoon salt; bring to boil. Reduce heat; cover and simmer until vegetables are soft, about 10 minutes. Stir in basil.

2 About 5 minutes before sauce is done, sprinkle scallops with black pepper and remaining ⅛ teaspoon salt. Heat remaining 2 teaspoons oil in large skillet over medium-high heat. Add scallops and cook, turning once, until lightly browned and opaque in center, 4–5 minutes.

3 Spoon sauce evenly onto 4 plates; top evenly with scallops. Spoon small amount of tapenade onto each scallop.

3 **SmartPoints value per serving** (4 scallops and ¾ cup sauce): 234 Cal, 8 g Total Fat, 1 g Sat Fat, 916 mg Sod, 26 g Total Carb, 9 g Sugar, 3 g Fib, 17 g Prot.

Thai shrimp in green curry sauce

serves 4   gluten free   under 20 minutes

5   ounces thin brown rice noodles

1   teaspoon canola oil

1   large red bell pepper, thinly sliced

1   zucchini, cut in half lengthwise
     and sliced

1   pound large peeled and
     deveined shrimp

1   (13-ounce) can light (reduced-fat)
     coconut milk

½   cup water

2   tablespoons Asian fish sauce

1   tablespoon green curry paste

1   teaspoon honey

6   scallions, thinly sliced

⅓   cup chopped fresh basil

Lime wedges

1 Prepare noodles according to package directions.

2 Meanwhile, heat oil in Dutch oven over medium-high heat. Add pepper and zucchini and cook, stirring often, until crisp-tender, about 3 minutes. Add shrimp, coconut milk, water, fish sauce, curry paste, and honey and bring to boil.

3 Stir in scallions. Cook just until shrimp are opaque in center, 1–2 minutes.

4 Divide noodles evenly among 4 bowls. Top evenly with curry and sprinkle with basil. Serve with lime wedges.

7 **SmartPoints value per serving** (1¼ cups soup and ½ cup noodles): 317 Cal, 9 g Total Fat, 4 g Sat Fat, 1,379 mg Sod, 37 g Total Carb, 5 g Sugar, 4 g Fib, 21 g Prot.

Pad Thai with tofu
and vegetables

Pad Thai with tofu and vegetables

serves 4   vegetarian

Many people reserve Pad Thai for takeout, thinking it much too complicated to attempt in their own kitchen. Nothing could be further from the truth. You can choose any protein you want as the basis of the dish; here it's tofu, but you may prefer chicken, shrimp, or even seitan. Be creative: This hearty main can be adapted to all tastes.

6	**ounces wide rice noodles**
¼	**cup tamarind juice**
¼	**cup soy sauce**
2	**teaspoons canola oil**
½	**pound green beans, trimmed and halved crosswise**
2	**carrots, shredded**
1	**small red onion, thinly sliced**
2	**garlic cloves, minced**
2	**teaspoons minced peeled fresh ginger**
1	**(14-ounce) package extra-firm tofu, drained and cubed**
1	**cup bean sprouts**
2	**tablespoons dry-roasted unsalted peanuts, chopped**
1	**scallion, thinly sliced**
	Chopped fresh cilantro
	Lime wedges

1 Cook rice noodles according to package directions.

2 Stir together tamarind juice and soy sauce in small bowl. Set aside.

3 Heat oil in wok or large skillet over medium-high heat until drop of water sizzles in pan. Add green beans, carrots, onion, garlic, and ginger. Stir-fry until vegetables are crisp-tender, 3–4 minutes.

4 Add tofu, rice noodles, bean sprouts, and tamarind juice mixture to wok. Stir-fry until noodles and tofu are heated through, 1–2 minutes. Sprinkle with peanuts, scallion, and cilantro. Serve with lime wedges.

7 **SmartPoints value per serving** (1¾ cups): 363 Cal, 10 g Total Fat, 1 g Sat Fat, 981 mg Sod, 54 g Carb, 7 g Sugar, 7 g Fib, 17 g Prot.

Let's do this together
To save time and make shopping easy, member Kylei Cucinella plans a week of dinners and she and her family eat the same seven evening meals every week for a month. She can shop from the same shopping list every week. "I'm all about saving time and money," she says. "You'd be surprised at how well you can eat on a budget!"

Singapore noodles with tofu and vegetables

serves 4   **gluten free**

Tofu, or bean curd as the Chinese call it, stars in this tasty dish filled with fresh produce. Try to make it in the spring, when asparagus and sugar snap peas are most likely to be available at the local farmers' market. A deep, rich sauce is the mainstay of this recipe, prepared with traditional Asian flavors such as fish sauce, rice vinegar, and hoisin. Vary the amount of these ingredients to your preference, and remember to garnish with cilantro and lime wedges at the end for a refreshing finish.

5	**ounces thin brown rice noodles**
3	**tablespoons water**
2	**tablespoons Asian fish sauce**
2	**tablespoons rice vinegar**
1	**tablespoon hoisin sauce**
2	**teaspoons curry powder**
2	**teaspoons tomato paste**
3	**teaspoons canola oil**
8	**ounces firm tofu, cut into ½-inch cubes**
1	**pound asparagus, trimmed and cut into 1½-inch pieces**
6	**ounces sugar snap peas, trimmed and halved crosswise**
6	**thin scallions, thinly sliced**
1½	**tablespoons minced peeled fresh ginger**
½	**cup chopped fresh cilantro**
	Lime wedges

1 Cook rice noodles according to package directions.

2 Meanwhile, stir together water, fish sauce, vinegar, hoisin sauce, curry powder, and tomato paste in small bowl.

3 Heat 2 teaspoons oil in large nonstick skillet over medium heat. Add tofu and cook, stirring often, until lightly browned, about 5 minutes. Transfer to plate. Add remaining 1 teaspoon oil to skillet. Add asparagus and cook, stirring often, 2 minutes. Add peas, scallions, and ginger and cook, stirring often, until vegetables are crisp-tender, about 2 minutes.

4 Add noodles and fish sauce mixture to skillet and cook, stirring constantly, until noodles are heated through, about 1 minute. Divide evenly among 4 plates, sprinkle with cilantro, and serve with lime wedges.

5 **SmartPoints value per serving** (2 cups): 266 Cal, 7 g Total Fat, 1 g Sat Fat, 872 mg Sod, 43 g Total Carb, 6 g Sugar, 6 g Fib, 12 g Prot.

Five-spice tofu and vegetable stir-fry

serves 4   vegetarian

½   **cup vegetable broth**

2   **tablespoons soy sauce**

1   **tablespoon rice vinegar**

1   **tablespoon Shaoxing (Chinese cooking wine) or dry sherry**

1½ **teaspoons cornstarch**

1   **teaspoon honey**

1   **tablespoon canola oil**

2   **garlic cloves, finely chopped**

1   **red pepper, thinly sliced**

2   **celery stalks, thinly sliced**

1   **(14-ounce) package extra-firm tofu, drained and cubed**

½   **teaspoon five-spice powder**

¼   **pound snow peas, trimmed**

1   **teaspoon Asian (dark) sesame oil**

1 Whisk together broth, soy sauce, vinegar, wine, cornstarch, and honey in small bowl until smooth.

2 Heat wok or large skillet over high heat until drop of water sizzles in pan. Add canola oil to wok and swirl to coat pan. Add garlic and stir-fry until fragrant, about 10 seconds. Add pepper and celery; stir-fry until crisp-tender, 2 minutes. Add tofu and five-spice powder; stir-fry until tofu is heated through, about 2 minutes.

3 Stir in broth mixture and snow peas; bring to boil. Reduce heat and cook, stirring constantly, until peas are bright green and sauce is slightly thickened, about 1 minute. Remove from heat and stir in sesame oil.

2 **SmartPoints value per serving** (1 cup): 183 Cal, 10 g Total Fat, 1 g Sat Fat, 541 mg Sod, 12 g Total Carb, 5 g Sugar, 4 g Fib, 13 g Prot.

Roasted tofu bowls with red pepper dressing

serves 4   **gluten free**   **vegetarian**

This is our kind of comfort food—robust, warming, and unfussy. Unlike many other recipes, which feature tofu cooked in broth, this time the tofu is roasted along with kale. Pumpkin seeds and pepper flakes provide the primary flavoring. The dressing is made with roasted red peppers, shallot, and garlic.

1	(14-ounce) package extra-firm tofu
4	teaspoons olive oil
½	teaspoon red pepper flakes
¼	cup pumpkin seeds
½	teaspoon plus ⅛ teaspoon salt
2	cups firmly packed baby kale
2	(8-ounce) packages frozen cooked quinoa
1	large shallot, finely chopped
1	garlic clove, minced
2	teaspoons balsamic vinegar
1	(6½-ounce) jar roasted red peppers packed in water (¾ cup), drained and roughly chopped
¼	teaspoon black pepper

1 Preheat oven to 450°F. Line large rimmed baking sheet with nonstick foil.

2 Pat tofu dry with paper towels and cut into 1-inch cubes. Add tofu to baking sheet, drizzle with 2 teaspoons oil, and toss to coat. Spread tofu in single layer. Sprinkle with pepper flakes, pumpkin seeds, and ¼ teaspoon salt. Roast until lightly browned, about 15 minutes.

3 Remove pan from oven and add kale to pan. Drizzle with ½ teaspoon oil; toss to coat. Return pan to oven and roast until kale wilts, about 5 minutes longer.

4 Meanwhile, microwave quinoa according to package directions; drain and transfer to large bowl. Keep warm.

5 To make dressing, heat 1 teaspoon oil in small skillet over medium-high heat. Add shallot and cook, stirring often, until softened and lightly browned, 2–3 minutes. Add garlic and cook, stirring constantly, until fragrant, about 30 seconds. Stir in vinegar. Transfer mixture to mini-food processor. Add peppers, remaining ½ teaspoon oil, and ⅛ teaspoon salt; pulse to finely chop.

6 Add 3 tablespoons of dressing, black pepper, and remaining ¼ teaspoon salt to quinoa and stir to combine. Divide quinoa mixture evenly among 4 plates. Top with tofu and kale mixture and any pumpkin seeds remaining in baking pan. Drizzle evenly with remaining dressing.

6 **SmartPoints value per serving** (about ¾ cup quinoa mixture, about ¾ cup tofu mixture, and about 2 teaspoons dressing): 361 Cal, 13 g Total Fat, 2 g Sat Fat, 441 mg Sod, 46 g Total Carb, 4 g Sugar, 7 g Fib, 19 g Prot.

Spiced edamame and green bean stew

serves 4   gluten free   vegetarian

3 teaspoons olive oil

1 onion, chopped

2 garlic cloves, minced

2 teaspoons tomato paste

2 teaspoons ground cumin

2 teaspoons ground coriander

1 (14½-ounce) can diced tomatoes

½ cup water

6 ounces green beans, trimmed and halved crosswise

2 cups frozen shelled edamame

¼ pound snow peas, trimmed and halved diagonally

½ teaspoon salt

¼ teaspoon black pepper

1 tablespoon chopped fresh parsley or cilantro

1 Heat 2 teaspoons oil in large nonstick skillet over medium heat. Add onion and cook, stirring often until lightly browned, about 5 minutes. Add garlic and cook, stirring constantly until fragrant, 30 seconds. Stir in remaining 1 teaspoon oil. Add tomato paste, cumin, and coriander and cook, stirring constantly, 1 minute.

2 Add tomatoes and water and bring to boil. Add green beans, reduce heat, cover, and cook, stirring occasionally, until crisp-tender, about 5 minutes.

3 Meanwhile, microwave edamame according to package directions; drain.

4 Add edamame, snow peas, salt, and pepper to skillet and cook, stirring constantly, until peas are bright green, about 1 minute. Remove from heat and sprinkle with parsley.

1 **SmartPoints value per serving** (1¼ cups): 207 Cal, 9 g Total Fat, 1 g Sat Fat, 471 mg Sod, 22 g Total Carb, 9 g Sugar, 7 g Fib, 12 g Prot.

Eat better

If you're not a fan of tofu, but would like to get more wholesome soy in your diet, try frozen shelled edamame. They have a delicate flavor, cook in just a few minutes, and can be used in stir-fries, soups, salads, and dips— and they're a great zero Points food!

Edamame tostadas

serves 4   gluten free   vegetarian

2   cups frozen shelled edamame

1   avocado, pitted, peeled,
      and mashed

¼   cup chopped fresh cilantro

2   scallions, finely chopped

2   tablespoons lime juice

1   garlic clove, crushed with a press

¼   teaspoon salt

¼   teaspoon red pepper flakes

4   (6-inch) corn tostada shells

2   cups shredded romaine lettuce

12   cherry tomatoes, sliced

¼   cup thinly sliced red onion

¼   cup plain fat-free yogurt

Cracked black pepper

1 Cook edamame according to package directions. Drain and rinse under cold running water until cool; drain again. Transfer to medium bowl and coarsely crush with potato masher. Stir in avocado, cilantro, scallions, lime juice, garlic, salt, and pepper flakes.

2 Spread edamame mixture evenly over tostada shells. Top evenly with lettuce, tomatoes, onion, and yogurt. Sprinkle with black pepper.

5 **SmartPoints value per serving** (1 tostada): 282 Cal, 15 g Total Fat, 2 g Sat Fat, 252 mg Sod, 27 g Total Carb, 7 g Sugar, 8 g Fib, 13 g Prot.

Eat better
Make the most of the flavorful edamame and avocado mixture. Use it as a pita filling or as a dip with fresh veggies.

Edamame
tostadas

Coconut-curry veggie rice bowls

serves 4   gluten free

1   **pound green beans, trimmed and halved crosswise**

1   **cup light (low-fat) coconut milk**

½   **cup vegetable broth**

1½   **tablespoons Asian fish sauce**

2   **teaspoons cornstarch**

1   **tablespoon Asian (dark) sesame oil**

2   **red bell peppers, thinly sliced**

1   **large carrot, cut into matchstick strips**

1½   **cups thawed frozen shelled edamame**

3   **garlic cloves, minced**

2½   **tablespoons Thai green curry paste**

2   **cups hot cooked brown rice**

¼   **cup thinly sliced fresh basil**

Lime wedges

1 Bring large saucepan of water to boil. Add green beans. Return to boil and cook until green beans are just crisp-tender, 2 minutes. Drain.

2 Whisk together coconut milk, broth, fish sauce, and cornstarch in small bowl. Set aside.

3 Heat oil in large skillet over medium-high heat. Add peppers and carrot. Cook, stirring occasionally, until vegetables are crisp-tender, 3 minutes. Add green beans and edamame; cook, stirring often, until heated through, 2 minutes. Add garlic and cook, stirring constantly, until fragrant, 30 seconds. Add coconut-milk mixture and cook, stirring constantly, until sauce comes to boil and thickens, about 1 minute.

4 Divide rice evenly among 4 bowls; top evenly with curry. Sprinkle with basil and serve with lime wedges.

7   **SmartPoints value per serving** (2 cups curry and ½ cup rice): 357 Cal, 13 g Total Fat, 5 g Sat Fat, 643 mg Sod, 50 g Total Carb, 7 g Sugar, 9 g Fib, 14 g Prot.

Adzuki-edamame salad with miso dressing

serves 4   **gluten free**   **vegetarian**   **under 20 minutes**

1   (10-ounce) package frozen
    shelled edamame

2   tablespoons orange juice

Grated zest and juice of 1 lime

2   tablespoons white miso

1   tablespoon olive oil

½   teaspoon grated peeled
    fresh ginger

1   (15-ounce) can adzuki beans,
    rinsed and drained

1   Kirby cucumber, halved
    lengthwise and sliced

2   carrots, coarsely shredded

2   tablespoons chopped red onion

2   tablespoons chopped
    fresh cilantro

1 Bring medium saucepan of water to boil. Add edamame and cook
5 minutes. Drain. Rinse under cold running water until cool; drain again.

2 Meanwhile, whisk together orange juice, lime zest and juice, miso, oil,
and ginger in large bowl until smooth. Add edamame, adzuki beans,
cucumber, carrots, onion, and cilantro; toss to combine.

2 **SmartPoints value per serving** (1½ cups): 255 Cal, 9 g Total Fat, 1 g Sat Fat,
683 mg Sod, 31 g Total Carb, 6 g Sugar, 8 g Fib, 15 g Prot.

Eat better

Add more zero Points veggies to
this salad if you have them on hand.
Halved grape tomatoes or diced red
bell pepper are good additions. You
can also serve the salad on top of
watercress, baby arugula, or baby
kale to get your greens!

**Capellini with
gingery vegetables**

Capellini with gingery vegetables

serves 4   vegetarian   under 20 minutes

6   ounces whole wheat capellini

2   teaspoons canola oil

2   tablespoons minced peeled
    fresh ginger

1   garlic clove, minced

4   cups small broccoli florets

1   red bell pepper, chopped

1   onion, thinly sliced

¼   cup sake

2   tablespoons hoisin sauce

2   cups thawed frozen shelled
    edamame

3   scallions, thinly sliced on diagonal

2   tablespoons soy sauce

2   tablespoons chopped
    unsalted peanuts

1 Cook capellini according to package directions.

2 Meanwhile, heat large wok or large skillet over medium-high heat until drop of water sizzles in it. Add oil and swirl to coat wok; then add ginger and garlic and cook, stirring constantly, until fragrant, 30 seconds. Add broccoli, bell pepper, and onion and cook, stirring constantly, until vegetables begin to soften, 2 minutes.

3 Add sake and cook until almost evaporated, 2 minutes. Stir in hoisin sauce and cook, stirring constantly, 2 minutes. Add edamame, scallions, and soy sauce and cook until heated through, 2 minutes longer.

4 Divide pasta evenly among 4 plates; top each serving evenly with vegetable mixture and sprinkle each serving with ½ tablespoon peanuts.

7 **SmartPoints value per serving** (1¼ cups): 396 Cal, 11 g Total Fat, 1 g Sat Fat, 597 mg Sod, 56 g Total Carb, 10 g Sugar, 10 g Fib, 20 g Prot.

Edamame and couscous salad with feta

serves 4   vegetarian

Switch out the ingredients in this recipe based on what you have on hand. You can use arugula instead of spinach, green beans instead of sugar snap peas, and cilantro or basil instead of mint.

1   cup couscous

1   cup vegetable broth

1⅓   cups frozen shelled edamame

6   ounces sugar snap peas, trimmed and halved lengthwise

3   teaspoons olive oil

6   scallions, thinly sliced

1   jalapeño pepper, halved lengthwise, seeded, and thinly sliced

2   teaspoons harissa

4   cups lightly packed baby spinach

Juice of ½ lime

2   tablespoons chopped fresh mint

¼   teaspoon salt

¼   teaspoon black pepper

¼   cup crumbled feta

Lime wedges

1 Cook couscous according to package directions, using vegetable broth instead of water (brands may vary on recommended amount of liquid). Fluff with fork and transfer to large bowl to cool slightly.

2 Meanwhile, bring medium saucepan of water to boil. Add edamame and cook until tender, about 5 minutes. Stir in peas. Drain immediately and rinse under cold running water until cool. Drain again.

3 Heat 2 teaspoons oil in large nonstick skillet over medium heat. Add scallions and jalapeño and cook until softened, about 2 minutes. Add harissa and cook, stirring constantly, until fragrant, 30 seconds. Remove skillet from heat. Stir in spinach just until slightly wilted. Add to couscous.

4 Add remaining 1 teaspoon oil, lime juice, mint, salt, and pepper to couscous mixture and toss to combine. Sprinkle with feta and serve with lime wedges.

7 **SmartPoints value per serving** (1 cup salad and 1 tablespoon feta): 333 Cal, 9 g Total Fat, 2 g Sat Fat, 501 mg Sod, 48 g Total Carb, 5 g Sugar, 7 g Fib, 15 g Prot.

Edamame and
couscous salad
with feta

Black bean–tomatillo dip

Black bean–tomatillo dip

serves 6 as an appetizer   **gluten free**   **no cook**   **vegetarian**   **under 20 minutes**

2   (15½-ounce) cans black beans, rinsed and drained

1   (12-ounce) can tomatillos, drained and coarsely chopped

1   tablespoon olive oil

1   (4½-ounce) can chopped green chiles

3   scallions, chopped

½   cup chopped fresh cilantro

2   tablespoons water

3   tablespoons lime juice

2   teaspoons chili powder

2   teaspoons ground cumin

½   teaspoon salt

½   teaspoon black pepper

Thinly sliced scallions and chopped fresh cilantro, for garnish (optional)

1 Combine beans, tomatillos, and oil in food processor and pulse until chunky puree forms.

2 Transfer bean mixture to large bowl and add remaining ingredients; stir until well combined, mixing in additional water if needed to reach desired consistency. Garnish, if desired.

1 **SmartPoints value per serving** (⅓ cup): 181 Cal, 3 g Total Fat, 0 g Sat Fat, 1,025 mg Sod, 29 g Total Carb, 1 g Sugar, 13 g Fib, 10 g Prot.

Eat better

Serve the dip with any fresh veggies you have on hand. Carrots, mini cucumbers, and radishes make a colorful and flavorful selection.

Chickpea and lemon bruschetta

serves 6 as an appetizer **vegetarian** **under 20 minutes**

1 **(15½-ounce) can chickpeas, rinsed and drained**

¼ **cup finely diced red onion**

1 **teaspoon grated lemon zest**

1 **tablespoon lemon juice**

2 **teaspoons extra-virgin olive oil**

1 **garlic clove, minced**

Pinch cayenne

1 **small (½-pound) whole wheat baguette**

¼ **teaspoon paprika**

1 With fork, coarsely mash chickpeas in medium bowl. Add onion, lemon zest and juice, oil, garlic, and cayenne; stir until combined.

2 Heat grill pan over medium-high heat. Cut off ends of baguette; discard or save for another use. Slice baguette on diagonal into 12 slices. Place slices of bread on pan and grill until well marked, about 2 minutes per side. Spread chickpea mixture evenly over bread and sprinkle with paprika.

3 **SmartPoints value per serving** (2 bruschetta): 168 Cal, 3 g Total Fat, 0 g Sat Fat, 311 mg Sod, 29 g Total Carb, 4 g Sugar, 5 g Fib, 7 g Prot.

Chickpea
and lemon
bruschetta

Black bean and goat cheese quesadillas

Black bean and goat cheese quesadillas

serves 4   vegetarian

6   **ounces white mushrooms, sliced**

1½   **teaspoons minced canned chipotles en adobo**

1   **cup rinsed and drained canned black beans**

1   **small tomato, chopped**

2   **scallions, thinly sliced**

½   **cup crumbled goat cheese**

¼   **cup chopped fresh cilantro**

4   **(7-inch) whole wheat tortillas**

¼   **cup light sour cream**

Lime wedges

1 Spray large skillet with nonstick spray and set over medium heat. Add mushrooms and cook, stirring, until mushrooms release their juice and it evaporates, about 8 minutes. Stir in chipotle. Transfer to plate and let cool slightly. Wipe skillet clean.

2 Layer one-fourth each of mushroom mixture, beans, tomato, scallions, goat cheese, and cilantro on half of each tortilla. Fold unfilled half of each tortilla over filling, pressing down lightly.

3 Spray same skillet with nonstick spray and set over medium-high heat. Place 2 quesadillas in skillet and cook until browned in spots, about 3 minutes. Spray quesadillas with nonstick spray and turn over. Cook until quesadillas are browned in spots and filling is heated through, about 2 minutes longer. Transfer to cutting board; keep warm. Repeat with remaining 2 quesadillas. Cut each quesadilla into 3 wedges and serve with sour cream and lime wedges.

6 **SmartPoints value per serving** (1 quesadilla and 1 tablespoon sour cream): 262 Cal, 7 g Total Fat, 3 g Sat Fat, 525 mg Sod, 38 g Total Carb, 4 g Sugar, 7 g Fib, 12 g Prot.

Lentil-beet burgers with kale pesto

serves 4   **vegetarian**

1   **small beet, trimmed and peeled**

1   **carrot**

1   **(9-ounce) package vacuum-packed cooked lentils**

¼   **cup whole wheat panko (bread crumbs)**

¼   **cup loosely packed fresh basil leaves**

1   **tablespoon Dijon mustard**

2   **small garlic cloves, minced**

½   **teaspoon plus ⅛ teaspoon salt**

¼   **teaspoon black pepper**

1   **teaspoon plus 1 tablespoon extra-virgin olive oil**

2   **cups baby kale**

2   **tablespoons pine nuts**

1   **teaspoon lemon juice**

1   **tablespoon freshly grated pecorino Romano**

2   **whole wheat hamburger buns, halved and toasted**

4   **slices tomato**

1   With shredding blade, shred beet and carrot in food processor. Replace shredding blade with chopping blade. Add lentils, panko, basil, mustard, 1 garlic clove, ½ teaspoon salt, and pepper; process until mixture is finely chopped and holds together. Shape into 4 (½-inch-thick) patties.

2   Heat 1 teaspoon oil in large nonstick skillet over medium heat. Add patties and cook, turning once, until lightly browned, about 8 minutes.

3   Meanwhile, to make pesto, rinse out food processor bowl and wipe with paper towels. Add 1 cup kale, pine nuts, lemon juice, remaining 1 garlic clove, and remaining ⅛ teaspoon salt and process until finely chopped. With motor running, drizzle in remaining 1 tablespoon olive oil. Add pecorino Romano and pulse to combine.

4   Place 1 bun half on each of 4 plates. Top each with ¼ cup kale, 1 burger, and 1 slice tomato. Top burgers evenly with pesto.

5   **SmartPoints value per serving** (1 open-face burger with generous 1 tablespoon pesto): 247 Cal, 9 g Total Fat, 1 g Sat Fat, 583 mg Sod, 34 g Total Carb, 5 g Sugar, 9 g Fib, 10 g Prot.

Cheesy corn and bean burgers

serves 4   **vegetarian**   **under 20 minutes**

1   **large egg**

1½   **teaspoons Mexican seasoning blend**

¼   **teaspoon salt**

¼   **teaspoon black pepper**

1   **(15-ounce) can black beans, rinsed and drained**

½   **cup frozen corn kernels, thawed**

½   **cup reduced-fat shredded pepper Jack cheese**

¼   **cup whole wheat dried breadcrumbs**

2   **tablespoons grated red onion**

2   **tablespoons chopped fresh cilantro**

2   **teaspoons canola oil**

4   **light whole wheat hamburger buns, split and toasted**

2   **tablespoons reduced-fat chipotle mayonnaise**

4   **slices tomato**

4   **green leaf lettuce leaves**

1 Whisk together egg, Mexican seasoning, salt, and pepper in medium bowl. Stir in beans and mash with potato masher or fork. Stir in corn, cheese, breadcrumbs, onion, and cilantro. Form into 4 (4-inch) patties.

2 Heat oil in large nonstick skillet over medium heat. Add patties and cook, carefully turning once with wide spatula, until browned and heated through, about 10 minutes.

3 Spread cut sides of hamburger buns with mayonnaise. Place burgers on bottoms of buns. Top evenly with tomato, lettuce, and tops of buns.

6   **SmartPoints value per serving** (1 burger): 322 Cal, 9 g Total Fat, 3 g Sat Fat, 1,005 mg Sod, 46 g Total Carb, 5 g Sugar, 15 g Fib, 18 g Prot.

Falafel sandwiches with avocado-lime sauce

serves 4   vegetarian

½   small avocado, pitted and peeled

2   tablespoons light sour cream

2   tablespoons chopped tomato

1   tablespoon minced red onion

1   teaspoon lime juice

¼   teaspoon salt

1   (15½-ounce) can pinto beans, rinsed and drained

¼   cup shredded reduced-fat Mexican cheese blend

¼   cup plain dried bread crumbs

2   scallions, thinly sliced

2   tablespoons chopped fresh cilantro

1   large egg white, lightly beaten

¼   teaspoon ground cumin

2   teaspoons canola oil

4   (7-inch) whole wheat pitas

1 To make sauce, mash avocado in small bowl. Add sour cream, tomato, onion, lime juice, and salt; stir to mix well.

2 Mash beans in large bowl. Add cheese, bread crumbs, scallions, cilantro, egg white, and cumin, stirring to mix well. With damp hands, form mixture into 4 (½-inch-thick) oval patties.

3 Heat oil in large nonstick skillet over medium heat. Add patties and cook until browned and crispy, about 3 minutes on each side.

4 Cut off top third of each pita and reserve for another use. Stuff each pita with 1 falafel patty and top with about 2 tablespoons avocado sauce.

5 **SmartPoints value per serving** (1 sandwich): 270 Cal, 10 g Total Fat, 2 g Sat Fat, 675 mg Sod, 37 g Total Carb, 2 g Sugar, 9 g Fib, 12 g Prot.

Eat better
Fill the pitas with any veggies you have on hand: Sliced cucumbers, cherry tomatoes, leaf lettuce, or sliced bell peppers would be delicious.

Falafel sandwiches with avocado-lime sauce

Moroccan vegetable stew

serves 4   gluten free   vegetarian

1 **teaspoon olive oil**
1 **onion, chopped**
1½ **teaspoons ground cumin**
1 **teaspoon curry powder,
   or to taste**
2½ **cups vegetable broth**
1 **(15½-ounce) can chickpeas,
   rinsed and drained**
1 **(14½-ounce) can diced tomatoes**
1 **large red bell pepper, chopped**
1 **zucchini, chopped**
¼ **teaspoon salt**
¼ **teaspoon black pepper**
4 **tablespoons plain fat-free yogurt**
Chopped fresh cilantro

1 Heat oil in large saucepan over medium-high heat. Add onion, cumin, and curry powder; cook, stirring often, until onion begins to soften, 2 minutes.

2 Add broth, chickpeas, tomatoes, bell pepper, zucchini, salt, and pepper and bring to boil. Reduce heat and simmer, partially covered, stirring occasionally, until vegetables are tender, about 12 minutes. Ladle evenly into 4 bowls; top with yogurt and sprinkle with cilantro.

1 **SmartPoints value per serving** (1½ cups): 175 Cal, 4 g Total Fat, 0 g Sat Fat, 1,022 mg Sod, 28 g Total Carb, 8 g Sugar, 8 g Fib, 10 g Prot.

Let's do this together

"I am an AVID meal planner! It has changed my life," says member Dcgirl23. Planning what she'll make for dinner six nights of the week saves time, money, and stress. "It's so easy to make the right choices when you have a plan and all the needed items at your fingertips!"

Carrot, snow pea, and bean stir-fry

serves 4   vegetarian

- **3   tablespoons soy sauce**
- **1   tablespoon unseasoned rice vinegar**
- **1   tablespoon mirin**
- **1   teaspoon Sriracha**
- **1   teaspoon cornstarch**
- **2   teaspoons Asian (dark) sesame oil**
- **2   scallions, thinly sliced**
- **3   garlic cloves, minced**
- **1   teaspoon minced peeled fresh ginger**
- **2   small carrots, thinly sliced**
- **1   small yellow bell pepper, thinly sliced**
- **6   ounces snow peas, trimmed**
- **1   (15-ounce) can adzuki beans, rinsed and drained**
- **¼   cup chopped fresh cilantro**

1 Whisk together soy sauce, rice vinegar, mirin, Sriracha, and cornstarch in small bowl. Set aside.

2 Heat oil in large nonstick skillet over medium heat. Add scallions, garlic, and ginger and stir-fry until scallion is softened, 2 minutes. Add carrots and stir-fry 1 minute. Add bell pepper and stir-fry until vegetables are almost crisp-tender, about 3 minutes. Add snow peas and stir-fry until bright green, 2 minutes.

3 Whisk soy sauce mixture again and add to skillet. Add adzuki beans and stir-fry until beans are heated through and sauce is thickened, about 2 minutes. Remove from heat and stir in cilantro.

1 **SmartPoints value per serving** (1 cup): 152 Cal, 3 g Total Fat, 0 g Sat Fat, 1,046 mg Sod, 25 g Total Carb, 4 g Sugar, 7 g Fib, 8 g Prot.

Lemony white bean, spinach, and rice bowls

Lemony white bean, spinach, and rice bowls

serves 2   gluten free   vegetarian   under 20 minutes

2   teaspoons olive oil

1   onion, chopped

3   garlic cloves, finely chopped

1   (15½-ounce) can cannellini (white kidney) beans, rinsed and drained

⅛   teaspoon red pepper flakes

6   ounces baby spinach

1½   cups cherry tomatoes, halved

2   teaspoons grated lemon zest

4   teaspoons lemon juice

Salt, to taste

1   (8.8-ounce) package ready-cooked brown rice

¼   cup freshly grated Parmigiano-Reggiano

1 Heat oil in large skillet over medium-high heat. Add onion and cook, stirring often, until tender, about 5 minutes. Add garlic and cook, stirring constantly, until fragrant, 30 seconds. Add beans and pepper flakes and cook, stirring constantly, until beans are heated through, about 2 minutes.

2 Add spinach and tomatoes and cook, stirring constantly, until spinach is wilted, about 2 minutes. Remove from heat and stir in 1 teaspoon lemon zest, 2 teaspoons lemon juice, and salt to taste.

3 Meanwhile, heat rice according to package directions. Transfer to medium bowl and stir in remaining 1 teaspoon lemon zest and remaining 2 teaspoons lemon juice.

4 Divide rice evenly between 2 bowls; top evenly with bean mixture. Sprinkle evenly with Parmigiano-Reggiano.

7 **SmartPoints value per serving** (generous ½ cup brown rice, ½ cup bean mixture, and 2 tablespoons cheese): 469 Cal, 9 g Total Fat, 3 g Sat Fat, 974 mg Sod, 76 g Total Carb, 6 g Sugar, 13 g Fib, 23 g Prot.

Chickpea and grilled vegetable salad

serves 4   vegetarian

4   **scallions**

2   **yellow squash, cut lengthwise into 4 slices**

2   **green or red bell peppers, quartered**

1   **cup whole wheat couscous**

1   **(15½-ounce) can chickpeas, rinsed and drained**

¼   **cup chopped fresh parsley**

1   **tablespoon extra-virgin olive oil**

2   **teaspoons grated lemon zest**

¼   **cup lemon juice**

½   **teaspoon salt**

¼   **teaspoon black pepper**

¼   **cup crumbled reduced-fat feta**

1 Spray grill rack with nonstick spray and preheat grill to medium-high or prepare medium-high fire.

2 Place scallions, squash, and bell peppers on grill rack and grill, turning, until vegetables are crisp-tender, about 10 minutes. Let cool slightly.

3 Cut vegetables into ½-inch pieces and transfer to large bowl.

4 Meanwhile, cook couscous according to package directions; add to vegetables. Add chickpeas, parsley, oil, lemon zest and juice, salt, and pepper and toss to mix well. Sprinkle with feta just before serving.

6 **SmartPoints value per serving** (about 1½ cups salad and 1 tablespoon feta): 342 Cal, 8 g Total Fat, 1 g Sat Fat, 696 mg Sod, 58 g Total Carb, 9 g Sugar, 13 g Fib, 15 g Prot.

Let's do this together

When you make this recipe, take a time-saving tip from member Nancy Kunak, who grills chicken, salmon, and veggies in batches for meals later in the week. "Grilled vegetables are good to eat cold or I use them in pasta dishes or salads," she says. And her grilled chicken and salmon stash goes into rice bowls, salads, or stir-fries.

Lemon-curry chickpea and celery salad

serves 6   gluten free   no cook   vegetarian   under 20 minutes

You can make this salad ahead and refrigerate it for up to 3 hours; longer than that and it becomes watery. Serve the salad on a bed of baby arugula or spinach and surround with halved cherry or grape tomatoes.

½   cup plain low-fat yogurt

1   teaspoon grated lemon zest

1   tablespoon lemon juice

2   teaspoons honey

1   teaspoon curry powder

½   teaspoon salt

2   cups sliced inner pale green celery stalks with leaves

1   (15½-ounce) can chickpeas, rinsed and drained

1   large carrot, cut into matchstick strips or shredded

3   scallions, sliced

Whisk together yogurt, lemon zest and juice, honey, curry powder, and salt in large bowl. Stir in celery, chickpeas, carrots, and scallions.

(1) SmartPoints value per serving (1 cup): 98 Cal, 2 g Total Fat, 0 g Sat Fat, 340 mg Sod, 16 g Total Carb, 7 g Sugar, 4 g Fib, 5 g Prot.

Lentil, strawberry, and
watercress salad

Lentil, strawberry, and watercress salad

serves 6   gluten free   no cook   vegetarian   under 20 minutes

2   tablespoons extra-virgin olive oil

2   tablespoons white balsamic vinegar

½   teaspoon salt

¼   teaspoon black pepper

2   small fennel bulbs with fronds attached

2   (9-ounce) packages vacuum-packed cooked lentils

1   pound strawberries, hulled and sliced

1   (4-ounce) package watercress

1 Whisk together oil, vinegar, salt, and pepper in large bowl.

2 Chop 2 tablespoons fennel fronds and add to bowl. Trim and thinly slice fennel bulbs and add to bowl. Add lentils and strawberries and toss gently to combine.

3 Place watercress on serving platter; top with salad.

2 **SmartPoints value per serving** (1 cup lentil mixture and about 1½ cups watercress): 195 Cal, 5 g Total Fat, 1 g Sat Fat, 244 mg Sod, 30 g Total Carb, 7 g Sugar, 11 g Fib, 9 g Prot.

Eat better
Because this salad is packed with zero Points ingredients, try sprinkling each serving with 1 tablespoon of crumbled feta cheese for only 1 additional SmartPoints.

Skillet ratatouille with eggs, page 163

chapter 4
Not just for breakfast: eggs

How to make the perfect omelette

As impressive as an omelette looks—and tastes—it's pretty simple to make. Here's how to make an omelette that's as good as the one at your favorite weekend brunch spot.

1 Get your fillings ready. Since the eggs are already cooked when the filling is added to an omelette, fillings should be heated or they should be foods that you don't mind eating only slightly warmed, like smoked salmon, cheese, chopped tomatoes, roasted red peppers, or scallions. For anything else, zap it in the microwave for a few seconds. See "Flavorful fillings" below for ideas and inspiration.

2 Whisk together the eggs and any seasonings you'd like (see Egg add-ins below). We like to use two whole eggs per omelette.

3 Make the omelette by heating 1 teaspoon canola or olive oil in a medium nonstick skillet over medium heat. Add the eggs and cook until almost set, about 3 minutes, gently lifting the edge of the eggs with a spatula to allow the uncooked portion of egg to flow underneath. When the egg is almost set, spoon the filling over half of the omelette and top with cheese, if using. Fold the unfilled portion of the omelette over the filling. Slide the omelette onto a plate and enjoy!

Flavorful fillings

Any of these make delicious omelette fillings (you'll need about a ½ cup of filling per omelette):

- Diced ham, cooked sausage, or crumbled cooked bacon
- Crabmeat or small cooked shrimp
- Thinly sliced smoked salmon
- Leftover cooked vegetables
- Fresh raw vegetables such as chopped tomatoes, thinly sliced scallions, or corn kernels
- Canned black beans or artichokes
- Salsa
- Chopped water-packed roasted red bell peppers
- Cooked grains such as rice or quinoa
- Small amounts of grated, shredded, or crumbled cheese

Egg add-ins

In addition to salt and pepper, try whisking one or more of these into the eggs before cooking:

- Chopped fresh herbs
- Seasoning blends like Cajun, Mexican, or Italian
- Hot sauce such as Sriracha or Tabasco
- Minced garlic or ginger
- Thinly sliced scallions

Add the fillings
to the omelette
when the eggs
are almost set,
then fold it
in half and slide
onto a plate.

Corn and pepper Jack frittata

serves 4   gluten free   vegetarian

6   **large eggs**

⅓   **cup part-skim ricotta**

½   **teaspoon ground cumin**

¼   **teaspoon salt**

¼   **teaspoon black pepper**

1   **cup thawed frozen corn kernels**

2   **scallions, sliced**

6   **tablespoons shredded pepper Jack**

1   **teaspoon canola oil**

12   **grape tomatoes, halved**

2   **tablespoons chopped fresh cilantro**

½   **cup refrigerated fat-free salsa**

1 Preheat broiler.

2 Whisk together eggs, ricotta, cumin, salt, and pepper in large bowl. Stir in corn, scallions, and 2 tablespoons pepper Jack.

3 Heat oil in medium nonstick skillet over medium heat. Add egg mixture and cook, lifting edges frequently with spatula to let uncooked egg flow underneath, until eggs are almost set, 2–3 minutes.

4 Top eggs with tomatoes, arranging cut side up; sprinkle with remaining 4 tablespoons cheese. Place skillet under broiler and broil frittata 5 inches from heat until cheese is melted and eggs are set, about 3 minutes.

5 Sprinkle frittata with cilantro and cut into 4 wedges. Serve hot, warm, or at room temperature with salsa.

(3) **SmartPoints value per serving** (1 frittata wedge and 2 tablespoons salsa): 245 Cal, 14 g Total Fat, 6 g Sat Fat, 485 mg Sod, 15 g Total Carb, 4 g Sugar, 2 g Fib, 17 g Prot.

Let's do this together
Member Anne Thalman makes frittatas every weekend. "Combine your choice of cooked veggies, add some seasoning blend and the eggs, and cook," she explains. "I cut them into wedges and portion them out for the whole week."

**Corn and pepper
Jack frittata**

Spinach-mushroom frittata with goat cheese

serves 4   gluten free   vegetarian

6   **large eggs**

½   **teaspoon salt**

¼   **teaspoon black pepper**

2   **teaspoons olive oil**

1   **(8-ounce) container sliced mushrooms**

1   **(6-ounce) bag baby spinach**

2   **plum tomatoes, sliced**

2   **ounces goat cheese, crumbled**

1 Preheat broiler.

2 Whisk together eggs, ¼ teaspoon salt, and pepper in large bowl.

3 Heat oil in 10-inch nonstick ovenproof skillet over medium heat. Add mushrooms and remaining ¼ teaspoon salt and cook, stirring occasionally, until lightly browned and most of liquid evaporates, about 8 minutes. Add spinach, in batches if necessary, and cook, stirring constantly, until wilted and most of liquid evaporates, about 2 minutes.

4 Pour egg mixture evenly over vegetables. Reduce heat and cook, without stirring, until eggs are set, 7–8 minutes.

5 Arrange tomato slices on top of eggs; sprinkle evenly with goat cheese. Place skillet under broiler and broil frittata 5 inches from heat until top is lightly browned, about 2 minutes. Cut into 4 wedges.

(2) **SmartPoints value per serving** (1 wedge): 196 Cal, 13 g Total Fat, 4 g Sat Fat, 435 mg Sod, 6 g Total Carb, 2 g Sugar, 2 g Fib, 15 g Prot.

Eat better

A large egg provides about 6 grams of protein, which is a good start toward the 46 grams per day that women need or the 56 grams needed by men.

Zucchini and tomato frittata

serves 4   *gluten free*   **vegetarian**

1   **tablespoon olive oil**
1   **onion, chopped**
3   **garlic cloves, minced**
2   **zucchini, diced**
1   **red bell pepper, diced**
½   **cup cherry tomatoes, halved**
⅓   **cup lightly packed thinly sliced fresh basil**
½   **teaspoon salt**
¼   **teaspoon black pepper**
4   **large eggs, lightly beaten**
⅓   **cup crumbled feta**

1 Preheat broiler.

2 Heat oil in 10-inch ovenproof nonstick skillet over medium heat. Add onion and cook, stirring, until softened, about 5 minutes. Stir in garlic and cook, stirring, until fragrant, about 30 seconds. Add zucchini, bell pepper, and tomatoes; cook, stirring, until vegetables are softened, about 6 minutes longer. Stir in basil, salt, and pepper.

3 Pour eggs evenly over vegetable mixture. Cook, without stirring, until eggs are almost set, about 5 minutes.

4 Sprinkle frittata with feta. Place skillet 5 inches from heat and broil until frittata is set and top is golden, about 3 minutes longer. Slide frittata onto serving plate and cut into 4 wedges. Serve hot, warm, or at room temperature.

3 **SmartPoints value per serving** (1 wedge): 176 Cal, 12 g Total Fat, 4 g Sat Fat, 504 mg Sod, 10 g Total Carb, 6 g Sugar, 2 g Fib, 10 g Prot.

Tomato and ricotta frittata

Tomato and ricotta frittata

serves 2   **gluten free**   **vegetarian**   **under 20 minutes**

2   **teaspoons olive oil**

1   **small (4-ounce) red potato, scrubbed and shredded**

½   **onion, chopped**

3   **large eggs**

¼   **teaspoon salt**

¼   **teaspoon black pepper**

⅓   **cup part-skim ricotta**

¼   **cup shredded part–skim mozzarella**

1   **tomato, seeded and diced**

1   **tablespoon minced fresh chives or chopped fresh basil**

1 Preheat broiler.

2 Heat oil in medium nonstick skillet over medium heat. Add potato and onion. Cook, stirring frequently, until vegetables are tender, about 4 minutes.

3 Meanwhile, beat eggs, salt, and pepper in medium bowl until frothy. Pour eggs over vegetables and reduce heat to medium. Cook, lifting edges frequently with spatula to let uncooked egg flow underneath, until eggs are almost set, 2–3 minutes.

4 Dot eggs with ricotta and sprinkle with mozzarella. Place skillet under broiler and broil frittata 5 inches from heat until top is lightly browned, about 2 minutes. Sprinkle with tomato and chives and cut into 4 wedges.

6   **SmartPoints value per serving** (2 wedges): 303 Cal, 17 g Total Fat, 6 g Sat Fat, 540 mg Sod, 17 g Total Carb, 4 g Sugar, 2 g Fib, 20 g Prot.

Eat better

To add more veggies to this frittata, throw in a small diced red bell pepper along with the potato and onion in step 2.

French country-style omelettes

serves 2   gluten free   vegetarian

2   teaspoons olive oil
1   small zucchini, thinly sliced
1   cup thinly sliced mushrooms
1   tomato, seeded and chopped
½   teaspoon dried thyme
¼   teaspoon salt
⅛   teaspoon black pepper
4   large eggs
1   tablespoon low-fat (1%) milk
¼   cup crumbled reduced-fat soft
     goat cheese
2   tablespoons snipped fresh chives

1 Heat 1 teaspoon oil in medium nonstick skillet over medium heat. Add zucchini, mushrooms, tomato, thyme, salt, and pepper; cook, stirring, until vegetables are softened, about 3 minutes. Transfer to plate.

2 Beat together eggs and milk in medium bowl.

3 Wipe skillet clean. Add remaining 1 teaspoon oil to skillet. Pour in half of egg mixture and cook until almost set, about 3 minutes, gently lifting edge of eggs with spatula to allow uncooked portion of eggs to flow underneath.

4 Spoon half of vegetable mixture over half of omelette. Top with 2 tablespoons goat cheese and 1 tablespoon chives. Fold unfilled portion of omelette over filling. Slide omelette onto plate and keep warm. Repeat with remaining egg mixture, vegetable mixture, cheese, and chives to make another omelette.

(3) **SmartPoints value per serving** (1 omelette): 268 Cal, 19 g Total Fat, 6 g Sat Fat, 430 mg Sod, 7 g Total Carb, 5 g Sugar, 2 g Fib, 18 g Prot.

Open-face egg and ricotta English muffins

serves 4   **vegetarian**   **under 20 minutes**

6   **large eggs**

1   **tablespoon chopped fresh chives**

1   **teaspoon chopped fresh thyme**

¼   **teaspoon salt**

⅛   **teaspoon black pepper**

1   **teaspoon olive oil**

½   **cup part-skim ricotta**

2   **whole wheat English muffins, split and toasted**

1 Beat eggs, chives, thyme, salt, and pepper in medium bowl until frothy.

2 Heat oil in large nonstick skillet over medium heat. Add egg mixture and cook, stirring, until eggs start to set, about 1 minute. Add ricotta and cook, stirring, until eggs are cooked through, about 2 minutes. Divide egg mixture evenly among muffin halves and serve.

4   **SmartPoints value per serving** (½ cup egg mixture and 1 muffin half): 228 Cal, 11 g Total Fat, 4 g Sat Fat, 438 mg Sod, 16 g Total Carb, 3 g Sugar, 2 g Fib, 16 g Prot.

Eat better

Place a large slice of tomato on each English muffin half before topping with the egg mixture, if you wish.

Shrimp, bell pepper, and thyme frittata

serves 4   gluten free

Frittatas are a great way to use up small amounts of ingredients that you have on hand. Diced cooked chicken breast, cooked salmon, or shrimp make delicious additions, and almost any vegetable or herb can be incorporated to make a quick and nourishing breakfast, lunch, or dinner.

4	**large eggs**
2	**teaspoons fresh thyme leaves**
2	**teaspoons chopped fresh chives**
¼	**teaspoon salt**
⅛	**teaspoon black pepper**
2	**teaspoons olive oil**
1	**small red bell pepper, diced**
1	**shallot, chopped**
4	**ounces cooked peeled and deveined shrimp, coarsely chopped**

1 Preheat broiler.

2 Whisk together eggs, thyme, chives, ⅛ teaspoon salt, and black pepper in medium bowl. Set aside.

3 Heat oil in 10-inch ovenproof skillet over medium heat. Add bell pepper and shallot; cook, stirring, until vegetables are softened, about 3 minutes. Add shrimp and remaining ⅛ teaspoon salt and cook just until heated through, about 1 minute.

4 Pour egg mixture over shrimp mixture. Cook, without stirring, until eggs are almost set, about 5 minutes.

5 Place skillet 5 inches from heat and broil until frittata is set and top is golden, about 5 minutes longer. Slide frittata onto serving plate and cut into 8 wedges. Serve hot, warm, or at room temperature.

① **SmartPoints value per serving** (2 wedges): 137 Cal, 8 g Total Fat, 2 g Sat Fat, 486 mg Sod, 3 g Total Carb, 2 g Sugar, 1 g Fib, 13 g Prot.

Shrimp, bell pepper, and thyme frittata

Egg, bacon, and greens
breakfast sandwiches

Egg, bacon, and greens breakfast sandwiches

serves 4

To quickly trim collard greens, fold each leaf in half at the stem, then tear off the tough portion of the stem and discard. To slice them, stack several leaves together, roll them up like a cigar, and thinly slice.

2	**teaspoons olive oil**
1	**shallot, thinly sliced**
½	**pound collard greens, trimmed and thinly sliced (about 6 cups)**
¼	**teaspoon salt**
¼	**teaspoon hot pepper sauce**
2	**slices turkey bacon**
4	**large eggs**
2	**whole wheat sandwich thins, split and toasted**
2	**tablespoons grated pecorino Romano**

1 Heat 1 teaspoon oil in large skillet over medium-high heat. Add shallot and cook, stirring constantly, until softened, about 2 minutes. Add greens and salt; cook, stirring frequently, until greens are tender, about 4 minutes. Stir in pepper sauce. Cover and keep warm.

2 Meanwhile, place bacon in large nonstick skillet; set over medium heat. Cook until crisp, about 3 minutes on each side. With tongs, transfer bacon to paper towel–lined plate and drain.

3 Add remaining 1 teaspoon oil to same skillet. Break eggs into skillet; cook until whites are opaque, 3–4 minutes. Cook, covered, until eggs are cooked as desired, 30–60 seconds longer.

4 Place a sandwich thin half, cut side up, on each of 4 plates. Top evenly with greens mixture. Break each slice of bacon in half and place on greens. Place an egg on top of bacon, sprinkle evenly with pecorino Romano, and serve at once.

3 **SmartPoints value per serving** (1 open-face sandwich): 192 Cal, 10 g Total Fat, 3 g Sat Fat, 466 mg Sod, 15 g Total Carb, 3 g Sugar, 5 g Fib, 12 g Prot.

Egg, asparagus, and prosciutto sandwiches

serves 2

2   tablespoons plain fat-free Greek yogurt

1½ tablespoons reduced-fat mayonnaise

2   teaspoons chopped fresh tarragon plus 2 tarragon sprigs for garnish

1   teaspoon grated lemon zest

1   tablespoon lemon juice

Pinch salt

Pinch cayenne

4   cups plus 1 tablespoon water

1   teaspoon apple cider vinegar

2   large eggs

14 thin asparagus spears, trimmed

2   (1-ounce) slices whole-grain country-style bread, toasted

2   thin slices prosciutto (about ½ ounce each)

Pinch red pepper flakes

1 To make sauce, whisk together yogurt, mayonnaise, chopped tarragon, lemon zest and juice, salt, and cayenne in small bowl until blended. Set aside.

2 To poach eggs, combine 4 cups water and vinegar in medium skillet and bring to boil. Reduce heat to bare simmer. Break 1 egg into cup. Holding cup close to water, slide egg into water. Repeat with remaining egg. Cook until whites are firm but yolks are still soft, about 5 minutes. With slotted spoon, transfer eggs, one at a time, to paper towel–lined plate to drain. Keep warm.

3 Meanwhile, put asparagus and remaining 1 tablespoon water in glass pie plate. Cover loosely with wax paper and microwave on High until crisp-tender, 3 minutes.

4 To serve, place 1 slice toast on each of 2 plates; top each with 7 asparagus spears. Place poached egg on top of asparagus and ruffle 1 slice prosciutto alongside. Spoon 2 tablespoons of sauce over each egg, sprinkle with red pepper flakes, and garnish each with tarragon sprig.

5 **SmartPoints value per serving** (1 open-face sandwich): 263 Cal, 13 g Total Fat, 4 g Sat Fat, 923 mg Sod, 18 g Total Carb, 4 g Sugar, 3 g Fib, 19 g Prot.

Egg, asparagus, and
prosciutto sandwiches

Egg and veggie sandwiches

serves 4   vegetarian   under 20 minutes

4   large hard-cooked eggs, peeled

6   tablespoons part-skim ricotta

2   tablespoons grated pecorino

2   tablespoons snipped fresh chives

¾   teaspoon salt

½   teaspoon grated lemon zest

¼   teaspoon black pepper

2   teaspoons olive oil

1   small red bell pepper, sliced

1   small yellow bell pepper, sliced

1   shallot, thinly sliced

2   small zucchini, halved lengthwise and sliced

2   (10-inch) ciabatta rolls, split

2   cups baby arugula

1 Preheat broiler.

2 Coarsely chop eggs. Combine eggs, ricotta, pecorino, chives, ¼ teaspoon salt, lemon zest, and ⅛ teaspoon pepper in small bowl.

3 Heat oil in large skillet over medium-high heat. Add bell peppers and shallot; cook, stirring often, until crisp-tender, 3–4 minutes. Add zucchini, remaining ½ teaspoon salt, and remaining ⅛ teaspoon pepper; cook, stirring often, until zucchini is tender, about 2 minutes.

4 Meanwhile, remove soft centers from each half of ciabatta. Place ciabatta, cut sides up, in broiler pan. Broil 4 inches from heat until lightly toasted, 1–2 minutes.

5 Spread cut sides of ciabatta evenly with egg mixture. Top evenly with arugula and vegetable mixture.

6 **SmartPoints value per serving** (1 open-face sandwich): 295 Cal, 12 g Total Fat, 4 g Sat Fat, 866 mg Sod, 32 g Total Carb, 4 g Sugar, 3 g Fib, 15 g Prot.

Let's do this together

No time to boil eggs? Buy them already cooked like member Dcgirl23 does. She enjoys them for a zero Points snack with some veggies or a piece of fruit and they're delicious for making sandwiches (like this one!) or tossed into salads.

Egg and avocado toasts with smoked salmon

serves 4   under 20 minutes

½   ripe avocado, pitted and peeled

2   tablespoons finely chopped red onion

2   teaspoons lime juice

½   teaspoon Dijon mustard

¼   teaspoon salt

⅛   teaspoon black pepper

4   large hard-cooked eggs, peeled and chopped

4   slices multigrain bread, toasted

1   cup baby arugula

2   ounces sliced smoked salmon

Lime wedges

1 Coarsely mash avocado in medium bowl; stir in onion, lime juice, mustard, salt, and pepper. Gently fold in eggs.

2 Top each bread slice with ¼ cup arugula. Top evenly with egg mixture and smoked salmon. Serve with lime wedges.

3 **SmartPoints value per serving** (1 open-face sandwich): 202 Cal, 10 g Total Fat, 2 g Sat Fat, 610 mg Sod, 15 g Total Carb, 2 g Sugar, 4 g Fib, 13 g Prot.

Eat better

To make perfect hard-cooked eggs, place the eggs in a large saucepan and add cold water to cover by 1 inch. Bring to a boil. Turn off the heat, cover, and let stand for 12 minutes. Drain and serve, or cool under cold running water and refrigerate in their shells for up to 1 week.

Indian scrambled eggs with cilantro naan

serves 2   **vegetarian**   **under 20 minutes**

If this spicy dish sounds like too much heat for a morning meal, it's perfect for a weekend brunch (double or triple the recipe if you have company) or a super-quick weeknight dinner. Stonefire is the brand of mini-naan we used.

4	**large eggs**
¼	**teaspoon salt**
⅛	**teaspoon black pepper**
3	**tablespoons chopped fresh cilantro**
3	**teaspoons canola oil**
1	**small garlic clove, crushed through a press**
2	**mini-naan**
1	**shallot, finely chopped**
1	**jalapeño pepper, halved lengthwise, seeded, and thinly sliced**
½	**teaspoon ground cumin**
⅛	**teaspoon ground turmeric**
1	**plum tomato, diced**

1 Whisk together eggs, salt, and black pepper in medium bowl until blended.

2 Stir together 1½ tablespoons cilantro, 1½ teaspoons oil, and garlic in small bowl.

3 Heat medium skillet over medium-high heat. Place 1 naan in skillet and cook, turning once, until well browned, about 1 minute. Remove from skillet and brush both sides with half of cilantro mixture. Repeat with remaining naan and remaining cilantro mixture. Cover to keep warm.

4 Heat remaining 1½ teaspoons oil in same skillet over medium heat. Add shallot and jalapeño; cook, stirring often, until softened, about 2 minutes. Add cumin and turmeric; cook, stirring constantly, until fragrant, about 30 seconds. Add tomato and cook until warmed, about 1 minute. Add egg mixture and cook, stirring often, until just set, 3–4 minutes.

5 Place naan on 2 plates and top evenly with egg mixture. Sprinkle evenly with remaining 1½ tablespoons cilantro.

5 **SmartPoints value per serving** (¾ cup egg mixture and 1 mini naan): 334 Cal, 19 g Total Fat, 4 g Sat Fat, 563 mg Sod, 24 g Total Carb, 4 g Sugar, 2 g Fib, 17 g Prot.

Bacon and egg fried rice

serves 4   gluten free   under 20 minutes

Make this comforting eggs-for-dinner meal with regular bacon instead of pancetta and with baby kale or arugula instead of spinach. If you prefer, you can lightly beat the eggs and scramble them in a skillet, then stir them into the rice mixture.

2   teaspoons canola oil

2   ounces diced pancetta

4   scallions, sliced

2   garlic cloves, minced

1   (5-ounce) container baby spinach

2   cups cooked brown rice

¾   cup frozen green peas

½   teaspoon salt

¼   teaspoon black pepper

4   large eggs

Cayenne pepper sauce, to taste

1 Heat large deep skillet or wok over high heat until drop of water sizzles in it. Add 1 teaspoon oil and swirl to coat pan. Add pancetta and stir-fry until crisp, about 1 minute. Add scallions and garlic; stir-fry until fragrant, about 15 seconds. Add spinach and stir-fry until wilted, about 1 minute. Add rice, peas, salt, and black pepper; stir-fry until hot, 1–2 minutes.

2 Meanwhile, heat remaining 1 teaspoon oil in large nonstick skillet over medium heat. Break eggs into skillet and cook until whites are opaque and yolks begin to set, 3–4 minutes.

3 Divide rice mixture among 4 plates; top each serving with 1 egg. Serve with pepper sauce.

7 **SmartPoints value per serving** (1 egg and generous ¾ cup rice): 311 Cal, 14 g Total Fat, 4 g Sat Fat, 519 mg Sod, 33 g Total Carb, 3 g Sugar, 4 g Fib, 14 g Prot.

Baby greens salad with
eggs and walnuts

Baby greens salad with eggs and walnuts

serves 4   gluten free   vegetarian   under 20 minutes

2   tablespoons apple juice

4   teaspoons extra-virgin olive oil

4   teaspoons apple cider vinegar

1   teaspoon coarse-grained mustard

½   teaspoon salt

¼   teaspoon black pepper

1   (5-ounce) container mixed baby salad greens

4   radishes, sliced

½   small red onion, thinly sliced

4   large hard-cooked eggs, peeled and quartered

¼   cup walnuts, toasted and chopped

1 To make dressing, whisk together apple juice, oil, vinegar, mustard, salt, and pepper in large bowl.

2 Add salad greens, radishes, and onion to dressing and toss to coat. Place salad on serving platter. Top with eggs and sprinkle with walnuts.

3 **SmartPoints value per serving** (about 1 cup salad, 1 egg, and 1 tablespoon walnuts): 179 Cal, 14 g Total Fat, 3 g Sat Fat, 392 mg Sod, 5 g Total Carb, 2 g Sugar, 1 g Fib, 8 g Prot.

Eat better
Turn this salad into a main dish by topping it with a grilled zero Points tuna steak or light tuna canned in water.

Roasted
asparagus and
red bell pepper
with dill, page 193

chapter 5
Fill your plate: veggies

How to add veggies to (almost!) anything

Want more vegetables in your everyday dishes? We've got easy techniques that you can use to sneak more into just about any dish.

Shred them.

Get out your grater or food processor and shred just about any firm or medium-firm veggie. Now they're easy to mix into other dishes from soups to slaws and meatloaf to muffin batter, and their finer form ensures they'll cook quickly. This works great for root vegetables like carrots, beets, and jicama; just about any kind of winter squash or summer squash; and even peeled broccoli stems. Try adding shredded carrot or squash to casseroles, shredded jicama or beet to slaws or tacos, and shredded zucchini to burger or meatloaf mixes.

Make a puree.

Boil just about any vegetable until it's tender, then whirl it in a food processor until you have a silky-smooth texture. Stir the puree into stews, casseroles, batters, sauces, and more to add great flavor and natural thickness. Purees of cauliflower, butternut squash, and carrot are mild and easy to use, but others, like beet, green pea, spinach, corn, and zucchini are great to experiment with. You can stir butternut squash puree into a sauce for mac and cheese, add cauliflower puree to soup for a natural creamy texture, and add corn puree to batter for corn bread and corn muffins. And a bit of beet puree is a favorite in some chocolate cake recipes!

Grill them.

Add extra vegetables anytime you're grilling outside or using a grill pan inside so you'll have them on hand for another meal. The wonderful caramelized flavors veggies take on over high heat make them perfect for adding to salads, sandwiches, tacos, quesadillas, and more. Some favorites for grilling include mushrooms, eggplant, broccoli, asparagus, corn on the cob, yellow squash, bell peppers, onions, and scallions. Grilled mushrooms are a favorite on burgers, grilled eggplant or bell peppers are a fabulous addition to just about any sandwich, and chopped grilled asparagus or scallions are terrific in omelettes.

Make ribbons.

Gadgets for turning your favorite veggies into deliciously thin strands are more popular than ever, but you can simply get out your peeler and make strips as well. Good candidates for ribbons include carrots, zucchini, yellow squash, winter squash, daikon, and beet. Most ribbons are excellent raw added to salads, or they can be sautéed for a pasta substitute or roasted until browned for a unique side dish or topping. Try zucchini ribbons under your favorite pasta sauce, daikon ribbons in a slaw, or sautéed beet ribbons as the base of a veggie-rich "noodle" bowl.

Pickle them.

It's easy! Save the brine from a bottle of store-bought pickles, or make your own quick-pickle base by heating vinegar, water, salt, and sugar until the sugar and salt dissolves. Pour the liquid into a jar, add vegetables, and refrigerate at least 1 day and up to a week. You can add zucchini and cucumber spears and onion slices raw; cauliflower florets, green beans, carrot sticks, fennel wedges, and small peeled beets should be blanched in boiling water for a few minutes and then cooled in cold water before adding. Use pickles in sandwiches, salads, and tacos, or dice them to use as a garnish for grilled meats, soups, dips, and more.

Use vegetable ribbons to make zero Points "pasta," salads, or side dishes.

Quick gazpacho

serves 6   gluten free   no cook   vegetarian

2   (14½-ounce) cans petite diced tomatoes

2   cups tomato-vegetable juice, chilled

1   red bell pepper, diced

1   English (seedless) cucumber, diced

1   jalapeño pepper, seeded and minced

1   small red onion, minced

1   tablespoon balsamic vinegar

¼   teaspoon salt

¼   cup chopped fresh basil

Stir together all ingredients except basil in large bowl. Set bowl inside another large bowl or sink filled with ice water and chill, stirring occasionally. (Or, refrigerate, covered, until chilled, about 4 hours.) Stir in basil just before serving.

1 **SmartPoints value per serving** (1½ cups): 58 Cal, 1 g Total Fat, 0 g Sat Fat, 429 mg Sod, 13 g Total Carb, 8 g Sugar, 3 g Fib, 3 g Prot.

Eat better
If you'd like, top this soup with cooked peeled and deveined shrimp for no additional SmartPoints value.

Quick gazpacho

Fresh pea soup with mint

serves 6   **gluten free**

Almost any herb works well in this soup. Try basil, dill, or chives instead of mint. Keep a batch of this soup in the refrigerator on hot summer days for a refreshing and out-of-the-ordinary afternoon snack.

2	**teaspoons unsalted butter**
1	**large leek, white and light green parts only, thinly sliced**
3½	**cups chicken broth**
2	**(9-ounce) packages frozen baby peas**
⅓	**cup fresh mint leaves**
½	**teaspoon salt**
¼	**teaspoon black pepper**
6	**tablespoons plain fat-free yogurt**

1 Heat butter in large saucepan over medium-high heat. Add leek, and cook, stirring often, until softened, about 2 minutes. Add 1 cup broth and bring to boil. Simmer until leek is tender, about 5 minutes. Add remaining 2½ cups broth and return to boil.

2 Add peas and cook just until crisp-tender, about 3 minutes.

3 Remove from heat and stir in mint, salt, and pepper. Let cool slightly and transfer in batches to blender and puree.

4 Ladle evenly into 6 bowls and top with yogurt. Soup may be served hot or chilled.

1   **SmartPoints value per serving** (1 cup soup and 1 tablespoon yogurt): 119 Cal, 3 g Total Fat, 1 g Sat Fat, 739 mg Sod, 16 g Total Carb, 7 g Sugar, 5 g Fib, 8 g Prot.

Arugula salad with walnuts and bacon

serves 6   gluten free   under 20 minutes

4   slices turkey bacon

1   tablespoon extra-virgin olive oil

1   tablespoon balsamic vinegar

1   tablespoon water

1   teaspoon Dijon mustard

¼   teaspoon salt

¼   teaspoon black pepper

1   garlic clove, minced

1   (5-ounce) package baby arugula

1   head Belgian endive, cut crosswise into 1-inch pieces

⅓   cup walnut halves, toasted and coarsely chopped

1 Cook bacon in medium nonstick skillet over medium heat until browned, about 4 minutes per side. Transfer to paper towels to drain. Crumble when cool.

2 Meanwhile, whisk together oil, vinegar, water, mustard, salt, pepper, and garlic in large salad bowl; add arugula, endive, walnuts, and bacon. Toss to coat.

3 **SmartPoints value per serving** (1⅓ cups): 111 Cal, 9 g Total Fat, 1 g Sat Fat, 246 mg Sod, 6 g Total Carb, 1 g Sugar, 3 g Fib, 4 g Prot.

Spanakopita
quesadillas

Spanakopita quesadillas

serves 4 as an appetizer   vegetarian   under 20 minutes

These make a quick and delicious lunch served with a cup of soup or a green salad. They're also terrific served with the Cucumber-yogurt sauce on page 11 instead of the marinara sauce.

½   **teaspoon olive oil**
½   **cup thinly sliced scallions**
1   **garlic clove, minced**
6   **ounces baby spinach**
½   **teaspoon dried oregano**
⅛   **teaspoon black pepper**
½   **cup crumbled feta**
2   **large flour tortillas**
¾   **cup marinara sauce, warmed**

1 Heat oil in large nonstick skillet over medium heat. Add scallions and garlic and cook, stirring often, until scallions are tender, about 1 minute. Add spinach and cook, tossing constantly, until spinach is wilted, about 2 minutes. Remove from heat and stir in oregano and pepper. Transfer to medium bowl and stir in feta. Wipe out skillet with paper towels.

2 Spoon spinach mixture evenly over one half of each tortilla. Fold unfilled half of each tortilla over filling and press down lightly.

3 Heat same skillet over medium heat. Lightly spray quesadillas with olive oil nonstick spray. Place quesadillas in skillet and cook, turning once, until crisp and heated through, about 4 minutes.

4 Cut each quesadilla into 4 wedges and serve with marinara.

(7) **SmartPoints value per serving** (2 quesadilla wedges and 3 tablespoons sauce): 218 Cal, 8 g Total Fat, 3 g Sat Fat, 634 mg Sod, 28 g Total Carb, 5 g Sugar, 4 g Fib, 8 g Prot.

Spinach and apple salad with blue cheese

serves 6   gluten free   no cook   vegetarian   under 20 minutes

1   **small shallot, minced**

2   **tablespoons lemon juice**

1   **tablespoon extra-virgin olive oil**

1   **tablespoon red-wine vinegar**

1   **teaspoon Dijon mustard**

½   **teaspoon salt**

¼   **teaspoon black pepper**

1   **(5-ounce) container baby spinach**

1   **large red apple, cored and thinly sliced**

⅓   **cup tart dried cherries**

¼   **cup crumbled reduced-fat blue cheese**

3   **tablespoons chopped toasted pecans**

1 In small bowl, whisk together shallot, lemon juice, oil, vinegar, mustard, salt, and pepper until blended.

2 Put spinach, apple, cherries, and blue cheese in large bowl. Pour dressing over salad and toss to coat. Sprinkle with pecans.

(4) **SmartPoints value per serving** (1⅓ cups salad and ½ tablespoon pecans): 118 Cal, 6 g Total Fat, 1 g Sat Fat, 297 mg Sod, 16 g Total Carb, 12 g Sugar, 3 g Fib, 3 g Prot.

Let's do this together
To make sure dinner gets under way as soon as possible, member Kam Szabo puts the menu for the week on a family white board. "Whoever gets home from work first knows what to start prepping," she says.

Spinach and apple
salad with blue cheese

Peach and endive salad with almonds

serves 4   gluten free   no cook   vegetarian   under 20 minutes

2   heads Belgian endive, thinly sliced lengthwise

2   peaches, halved, pitted, and cut into wedges

3   tablespoons water

1   tablespoon champagne vinegar or apple cider vinegar

2   teaspoons extra-virgin olive oil

2   teaspoons coarse-grained Dijon mustard

¼   teaspoon salt

¼   teaspoon black pepper

2   cups lightly packed spring mix lettuces with fresh herbs

¼   cup sliced almonds, toasted

¼   cup crumbled goat cheese

1 Combine endive and peaches in medium bowl.

2 To make dressing, whisk together water, vinegar, oil, mustard, salt, and pepper in small bowl. Drizzle over peaches and endive; toss until coated evenly.

3 Divide spring mix lettuces evenly among 4 plates. Top evenly with peach-endive mixture and sprinkle evenly with almonds and goat cheese.

3 **SmartPoints value per serving** (about 1¼ cups salad, 1 tablespoon almonds, and 1 tablespoon cheese): 170 Cal, 9 g Total Fat, 2 g Sat Fat, 233 mg Sod, 19 g Total Carb, 8 g Sugar, 10 g Fib, 7 g Prot.

Eat better

Since this salad is made from mostly zero Points ingredients, we've included higher SmartPoints value nuts and cheese to make a salad that tastes like a treat.

Grilled bell peppers with olive vinaigrette

serves 6   gluten free   vegetarian   under 20 minutes

This olive vinaigrette tastes great on any kind of grilled vegetables or fish or as the dressing for a Greek salad. Try it made with green olives, too, for another bold-flavored option.

1	**tablespoon water**
1	**teaspoon extra-virgin olive oil**
4	**teaspoons red-wine vinegar**
¼	**teaspoon salt**
¼	**teaspoon red pepper flakes**
⅓	**cup pitted Kalamata olives, finely chopped**
6	**assorted color bell peppers, halved**
¼	**cup chopped fresh basil**

1 Spray grill rack with nonstick spray; preheat grill to medium or prepare medium fire.

2 To make vinaigrette, whisk together water, oil, vinegar, salt, and pepper flakes in small bowl. Stir in olives. Set aside.

3 Lightly spray peppers with olive oil nonstick spray. Place peppers on grill rack; cook, turning once, until tender and slightly charred, 10–12 minutes.

4 Thickly slice peppers and arrange on platter. Stir basil into vinaigrette and spoon over peppers. Serve warm or at room temperature.

1 **SmartPoints value per serving** (about ½ cup): 42 Cal, 2 g Total Fat, 0 g Sat Fat, 154 mg Sod, 6 g Total Carb, 3 g Sugar, 2 g Fib, 1 g Prot.

Cucumber, honeydew,
and pepitas salad

Cucumber, honeydew, and pepitas salad

serves 4   gluten free   no cook   vegetarian   under 20 minutes

The sweet and savory combination of melon and cucumber make this a perfect addition to any summer meal. Try cantaloupe or Crenshaw melon instead of honeydew to add a twist of orange color to the salad. If you can't find pepitas, sunflower seeds are a good substitute.

½ cup plain low-fat yogurt

Grated zest and juice of ½ lime

½ teaspoon ground cumin

½ teaspoon salt

Pinch cayenne

2 cups honeydew melon chunks

⅓ cup sliced English (seedless) cucumber

⅓ cup fresh cilantro leaves

¼ cup thinly sliced red onion

8 small leaves red leaf lettuce or Bibb lettuce

2 tablespoons pepitas (green pumpkin seeds), toasted

1 To make dressing, whisk together yogurt, lime zest and juice, cumin, salt, and cayenne in small bowl.

2 Place honeydew, cucumber, cilantro, and onion in medium bowl; toss to combine.

3 Arrange lettuce leaves evenly on 4 salad plates. Top with honeydew mixture, and drizzle with dressing. Sprinkle with pepitas.

1 **SmartPoints value per serving** (2 lettuce leaves, about ⅔ cup salad, and 2 tablespoons dressing): 70 Cal, 1 g Total Fat, 0 g Sat Fat, 331 mg Sod, 13 g Carb, 10 g Sugar, 2 g Fib, 3 g Prot.

Green salad with carrot vinaigrette

serves 4　　**no cook**　　**vegetarian**　　**under 20 minutes**

3	tablespoons finely shredded carrot
1	teaspoon grated peeled fresh ginger
1½	tablespoons seasoned rice vinegar
1	tablespoon Asian (dark) sesame oil
1	tablespoon water
½	teaspoon soy sauce
¼	teaspoon salt
1	large head Boston lettuce, leaves torn
1	small Kirby cucumber, thinly sliced
½	cup cherry tomatoes, halved
2	scallions, thinly sliced

1 Puree carrot, ginger, vinegar, oil, water, soy sauce, and salt in blender or mini–food processor.

2 Combine lettuce, cucumber, tomatoes, and scallions in large bowl. Drizzle with dressing and toss to coat.

2 **SmartPoints value per serving** (2 cups): 47 Cal, 4 g Total Fat, 1 g Sat Fat, 190 mg Sod, 3 g Total Carb, 2 g Sugar, 1 g Fib, 1 g Prot.

Eat better
Turn this salad into a main dish by tossing in zero Points foods such as cooked skinless boneless chicken breast, shrimp, or shelled edamame.

Green bean salad with ricotta salata

serves 6   **gluten free**   **vegetarian**   **under 20 minutes**

This salad is delicious with sugar snap peas instead of green beans. Cook sugar snaps only for about 1 minute. Serve this dish in a large bowl or on a platter for a colorful centerpiece of any meal.

1	**pound slender green beans, trimmed and halved**
½	**pound plum tomatoes, diced**
3	**mini-cucumbers, thinly sliced**
1	**red onion, thinly sliced**
¼	**cup lightly packed fresh mint leaves, thinly sliced**

Grated zest and juice of 1 lemon

1	**tablespoon extra-virgin olive oil**
½	**teaspoon salt**
¼	**teaspoon black pepper**
⅓	**cup coarsely grated ricotta salata**

1 Bring large saucepan of lightly salted water to boil. Add green beans; return to boil and cook 3 minutes. Drain beans; rinse under cool running water and drain again.

2 Combine green beans, tomatoes, cucumbers, onion, mint, lemon zest and juice, oil, salt, and pepper in serving bowl. Toss until coated evenly. Sprinkle with ricotta salata.

(2) **SmartPoints value per serving** (about 1 cup salad and scant 1 tablespoon cheese): 96 Cal, 5 g Total Fat, 2 g Sat Fat, 321 mg Sod, 11 g Total Carb, 4 g Sugar, 4 g Fib, 4 g Prot.

Greek salad with feta and artichokes

serves 4   gluten free   no cook   vegetarian   under 20 minutes

1   garlic clove, halved

1   teaspoon grated lemon zest

3   tablespoons lemon juice

1   tablespoon extra-virgin olive oil

1   teaspoon dried oregano

¼   teaspoon salt

¼   teaspoon black pepper

4   cups sliced romaine lettuce

2   cups baby arugula

1   (14-ounce) can quartered artichoke hearts in water, drained

1   large Kirby cucumber, halved lengthwise and sliced

1   small yellow or red bell pepper, quartered and sliced

1   cup grape tomatoes, halved

¼   cup sliced red onion

6   pitted Kalamata olives, cut into slivers

½   cup crumbled reduced-fat feta

Rub inside of large salad bowl with cut sides of garlic clove; discard garlic. Add lemon zest and juice, oil, oregano, salt, and pepper to bowl; whisk until blended. Add romaine, arugula, artichoke hearts, cucumber, bell pepper, tomatoes, onion, and olives and toss to coat. Sprinkle with feta and serve.

2 **SmartPoints value per serving** (2¼ cups salad and 2 tablespoons feta): 128 Cal, 7 g Total Fat, 2 g Sat Fat, 675 mg Sod, 16 g Total Carb, 4 g Sugar, 6 g Fib, 7 g Prot.

Let's do this together

Make salads like this one even quicker by pre-prepping the veggies. "I take one day a week to wash and chop all fruits and vegetables so they are ready to eat at a moment's notice," says member Brianna Engebretsen. "If it's all made, I have no excuses."

Greek salad
with feta and
artichokes

Spicy butternut squash, apple, and raisin slaw

Spicy butternut squash, apple, and raisin slaw

serves 6   gluten free   no cook   vegetarian   under 20 minutes

Raw butternut squash lends a sweet and nutty flavor to this slaw. If you're skeptical, carrots make a great substitute. Use the food processor to make quick work of shredding either one.

¼   cup light (low-fat) coconut milk

1   tablespoon grated peeled fresh ginger

Grated zest and juice of 1 lime

2   teaspoons packed light brown sugar

1   teaspoon harissa, or to taste

¼   teaspoon salt

1   (1½-pound) butternut squash, peeled, seeded, and coarsely shredded (6 cups)

1   large Granny Smith apple, unpeeled, cored, and cut into matchsticks

¼   cup golden raisins, chopped

2   tablespoons shredded unsweetened coconut, toasted

1   To make dressing, whisk together coconut milk, ginger, lime zest and juice, brown sugar, harissa, and salt in large bowl.

2   Add squash, apple, and raisins; toss to coat evenly. Serve sprinkled with coconut.

(2) **SmartPoints value per serving** (about 1 cup): 104 Cal, 2 g Total Fat, 1 g Sat Fat, 116 mg Sod, 24 g Total Carb, 11 g Sugar, 4 g Fib, 1 g Prot.

Microwave broccoli with spicy garlic oil

serves 4 **gluten free** **vegetarian** **under 20 minutes**

1 **(12-ounce) package broccoli florets**
2 **tablespoons water**
4 **teaspoons olive oil**
1 **large garlic clove, minced**
¼ **teaspoon red pepper flakes**
¼ **teaspoon salt**
Lemon wedges

1 Combine broccoli and water in large microwavable bowl. Cover with wax paper and microwave on High until broccoli is crisp-tender, 3–3½ minutes, stirring once halfway through cooking. Drain. Return broccoli to same bowl.

2 Meanwhile, heat oil in small skillet over medium heat. Add garlic and pepper flakes and cook, stirring constantly, until fragrant, about 30 seconds. Add oil mixture and salt to broccoli; toss to coat. Serve with lemon wedges.

1 **SmartPoints value per serving** (1 cup): 65 Cal, 5 g Total Fat, 1 g Sat Fat, 168 mg Sod, 5 g Total Carb, 1 g Sugar, 2 g Fib, 3 g Prot.

Eat better
This recipe proves it takes nearly no time to cook fresh, flavorful veggies for dinner. Try tossing the broccoli with cooked rice or pasta to make a quick and simple main dish.

Cabbage salad with lime-Sriracha dressing

serves 6   **gluten free**   **no cook**   **under 20 minutes**

Serve this Asian-inspired salad alongside sandwiches, with grilled salmon or chicken, or use it as a filling for wraps. It does have a kick, so if you're serving it to kids, hold back on the Sriracha.

5   **cups finely shredded Napa cabbage**

4   **mini cucumbers, quartered lengthwise and sliced**

1   **green bell pepper, cut into ¼-inch dice**

⅓   **cup chopped fresh cilantro**

½   **small red onion, finely chopped**

2   **tablespoons lime juice**

2   **tablespoons grated peeled fresh ginger**

1½   **tablespoons Asian fish sauce**

1   **tablespoon packed brown sugar**

2   **teaspoons Asian (dark) sesame oil**

1   **teaspoon Sriracha**

1 Toss together cabbage, cucumbers, bell pepper, cilantro, and onion in large bowl.

2 To make dressing, whisk together all remaining ingredients in small bowl. Pour dressing over cabbage mixture and toss until coated. Serve at once or refrigerate, covered, up to overnight. For best flavor, let salad stand at room temperature for about 1 hour before serving.

1 **SmartPoints value per serving** (1⅓ cups): 67 Cal, 2 g Total Fat, 0 g Sat Fat, 385 mg Sod, 12 g Total Carb, 7 g Sugar, 3 g Fib, 2 g Prot.

Roasted asparagus
and red bell pepper
with dill

Roasted asparagus and red bell pepper with dill

serves 4   gluten free   vegetarian

1   **pound asparagus, trimmed**
1   **large red bell pepper, cut into ½-inch strips**
1   **teaspoon lemon zest**
1   **tablespoon lemon juice**
2   **teaspoons extra-virgin olive oil**
½   **teaspoon salt**
¼   **teaspoon red pepper flakes**
1   **tablespoon chopped fresh dill**

1   Preheat oven to 425°F. Spray large rimmed baking sheet with nonstick spray.

2   Place asparagus and bell pepper on baking sheet and lightly spray with olive oil nonstick spray. Toss to coat. Arrange vegetables in single layer on baking sheet. Bake until crisp-tender, shaking pan occasionally, about 10 minutes for asparagus and about 15 minutes for bell pepper.

3   Meanwhile, to make dressing, stir together lemon zest and juice, oil, salt, and pepper flakes in small bowl.

4   Place asparagus on platter; top with bell pepper. Drizzle with dressing and sprinkle with dill. Serve warm or at room temperature.

1 **SmartPoints value per serving** (scant ⅔ cup): 56 Cal, 3 g Total Fat, 0 g Sat Fat, 294 mg Sod, 7 g Total Carb, 4 g Sugar, 3 g Fib, 3 g Prot.

Stir-fried ginger spinach

serves 4   vegetarian   under 20 minutes

1   teaspoon Asian (dark) sesame oil

1   garlic clove, minced

½   teaspoon minced peeled
        fresh ginger

1   (10-ounce) bag prewashed
        spinach, torn into bite-size pieces

1   tablespoon soy sauce

1   tablespoon rice vinegar

Pinch red pepper flakes

1 Heat large skillet over medium-high heat until hot. Add oil, swirl to coat pan, then add garlic and ginger. Cook, stirring constantly, until fragrant, about 15 seconds.

2 Add spinach, soy sauce, vinegar, and pepper flakes; cook, stirring constantly, until spinach is just wilted, about 2 minutes. Serve at once.

0 **SmartPoints value per serving** (⅓ cup): 30 Cal, 1 g Total Fat, 0 g Sat Fat, 274 mg Sod, 3 g Total Carb, 0 g Sugar, 2 g Fib, 2 g Prot.

Let's do this together
Make this super-quick side dish even faster with a tip from member Dr. Ronald E. Hunter Jr. "I buy fresh ginger in a tube and use precut garlic to make meal prep faster," he says.

Roasted bell peppers and radicchio

serves 4   gluten free   vegetarian

1   red bell pepper, cut into eighths

1   yellow bell pepper, cut into eighths

1   head radicchio, cut into 8 wedges

1   medium red onion, cut into eighths

1½ tablespoons chopped fresh rosemary, or 1½ teaspoons dried, crumbled

1   tablespoon olive oil

¾   teaspoon salt

¼   teaspoon black pepper

1 Preheat oven to 500°F. Spray large rimmed baking sheet with nonstick spray.

2 Combine all ingredients in large bowl; toss to coat. Arrange vegetables on baking pan in single layer. Roast until lightly browned, 13–15 minutes, stirring once halfway through.

1 **SmartPoints value per serving** (1 cup): 88 Cal, 4 g Total Fat, 1 g Sat Fat, 468 mg Sod, 13 g Total Carb, 3 g Sugar, 3 g Fib, 3 g Prot.

Eat better
Double up on this recipe and enjoy the leftovers as a salad for lunch the next day. Add 1 tablespoon crumbled goat cheese to each serving for 1 additional SmartPoints value.

Corn, zucchini, and tomatoes with cilantro

serves 4   gluten free   vegetarian

1   tablespoon olive oil

1   onion, chopped

1   garlic clove, minced

1   jalapeño pepper, seeded and minced

1½ cups fresh corn kernels (from 2 ears or use 10-ounce package frozen corn kernels)

1   zucchini, chopped

1   red bell pepper, chopped

1   teaspoon ground cumin

1   cup cherry tomatoes, halved

2   tablespoons chopped cilantro

1   tablespoon lime juice

¾   teaspoon salt

¼   teaspoon black pepper

1 Heat oil in large skillet over medium-high heat; add onion, garlic, and jalapeño. Cook, stirring often, until softened, about 5 minutes.

2 Add corn, zucchini, bell pepper, and cumin; cook, stirring often, until softened, 7–8 minutes. Stir in cherry tomatoes and cook just until warmed through, about 1 minute.

3 Remove from heat and stir in cilantro, lime juice, salt, and pepper.

1 **SmartPoints value per serving** (1 cup): 130 Cal, 4 g Total Fat, 1 g Sat Fat, 447 mg Sod, 23 g Total Carb, 7 g Sugar, 4 g Fib, 4 g Prot.

Eat better

To make a company-worthy dinner, spoon the veggies onto a plate, then top with a zero Points grilled salmon fillet or skinless boneless chicken breast.

Corn, zucchini, and tomatoes with cilantro

Green bean and tomato sauté

Green bean and tomato sauté

serves 4   **gluten free**   **vegetarian**

1   **pound green beans, trimmed and halved**

1   **tablespoon olive oil**

2   **garlic cloves, minced**

1   **large shallot, finely chopped**

1½ **cups cherry tomatoes, halved**

1   **teaspoon balsamic vinegar**

½   **teaspoon salt**

⅛   **teaspoon black pepper**

3   **tablespoons chopped fresh basil**

1 Bring large pot of lightly salted water to boil. Add green beans and cook until crisp-tender, about 3 minutes. Drain.

2 Meanwhile, heat oil in large skillet over medium-high heat. Add garlic and shallot and cook, stirring constantly, until fragrant, about 1 minute. Add tomatoes and cook until heated through, about 2 minutes. Add green beans, vinegar, salt, and pepper to skillet and toss to coat. Remove from heat and stir in basil.

1 **SmartPoints value per serving** (1 cup): 87 Cal, 4 g Total Fat, 0 g Sat Fat, 303 mg Sod, 13 g Total Carb, 4 g Sugar, 5 g Fib, 3 g Prot.

Parmesan-basil broiled tomatoes

serves 4   gluten free   vegetarian

8   **plum or other small tomatoes,
     halved lengthwise**

1   **tablespoon chopped fresh thyme**

2   **teaspoons extra-virgin olive oil**

½   **teaspoon salt**

½   **teaspoon black pepper**

2   **tablespoons freshly grated
     Parmigiano-Reggiano**

2   **tablespoons chopped fresh basil**

1 Preheat broiler and spray large rimmed baking sheet with nonstick spray.

2 Toss together tomatoes, thyme, oil, salt, and pepper in large bowl. Arrange tomatoes on pan. Broil 6 inches from heat until tomatoes are tender and lightly charred, about 5 minutes on each side. Sprinkle with Parmigiano-Reggiano; broil until cheese melts, about 1 minute.

3 Transfer tomatoes to platter; sprinkle with basil.

1 **SmartPoints value per serving** (4 tomato halves): 55 Cal, 3 g Total Fat, 1 g Sat Fat, 331 mg Sod, 5 g Total Carb, 3 g Sugar, 2 g Fib, 2 g Prot.

Eat better
Since this dish is made with mostly zero Points ingredients, we've used 2 tablespoons of flavorful Parmigiano-Reggiano cheese to top the tomatoes. Genuine Parmigiano-Reggiano comes from the Emilia-Romagna region of Italy; it's made from the milk of grass-fed cows and aged at least 12 months. Its unparalleled taste is worth the SmartPoints!

Parmesan-basil broiled tomatoes

Minted zucchini and cherry tomatoes

serves 4   gluten free   vegetarian   under 20 minutes

This fresh, simple recipe is an easy way to combine two ordinary vegetables to make a delicious side dish. Instead of mint, you can use chopped fresh basil, dill, or tarragon. If you're using tarragon, start by adding just 2 teaspoons.

1	teaspoon olive oil
3	zucchini, diced
1	garlic clove, minced
1	cup cherry tomatoes, halved
¼	teaspoon salt
⅛	teaspoon black pepper
2	tablespoons chopped fresh mint

1 Heat oil in large nonstick skillet over medium heat. Add zucchini and garlic; cook, stirring frequently, until crisp-tender, 1–2 minutes.

2 Stir in tomatoes, salt, and pepper; cook, stirring constantly, until tomatoes are heated through, about 1 minute. Remove from heat; stir in mint.

0 **SmartPoints value per serving** (about ¾ cup): 43 Cal, 2 g Total Fat, 0 g Sat Fat, 160 mg Sod, 7 g Total Carb, 5 g Sugar, 2 g Fib, 2 g Prot.

Zucchini-avocado salad

serves 4   **gluten free**   **no cook**   **vegetarian**   **under 20 minutes**

A too-soft avocado will be difficult to cut into neat slices for this recipe. Ripe avocados should just yield to gentle pressure in the palm of your hand.

4	**teaspoons extra-virgin olive oil**
½	**teaspoon grated lemon zest**
1	**tablespoon lemon juice**
¼	**teaspoon salt**
⅛	**teaspoon black pepper**
2	**small zucchini, thinly sliced on diagonal**
1	**ripe avocado, pitted, peeled, and sliced**
2	**tablespoons whole roasted unsalted almonds, finely chopped**

Lemon wedges

1 To make dressing, whisk together oil, lemon zest and juice, salt, and pepper in small bowl.

2 Arrange one quarter of zucchini and avocado slices in concentric circles on each of 4 plates; drizzle evenly with dressing and sprinkle with almonds. Serve with lemon wedges.

5 **SmartPoints value per serving** (1 salad): 158 Cal, 14 g Total Fat, 2 g Sat Fat, 154 mg Sod, 7 g Total Carb, 2 g Sugar, 4 g Fib, 3 g Prot.

Zucchini
fries

Zucchini fries

serves 4   vegetarian

In addition to zucchini, use this "frying" technique for yellow squash or eggplant. It also works well with thick-cut onion rings or sliced green tomatoes. Serve them with steaks or burgers or as an appetizer.

1½ **tablespoons all-purpose flour**

1   **teaspoon Italian seasoning**

¾   **teaspoon salt**

¾   **cup panko (bread crumbs)**

1   **tablespoon olive oil**

2   **large egg whites**

2   **zucchini, cut into 3 x ½-inch pieces**

Lemon wedges

1 Preheat oven to 425ºF. Line large rimmed baking sheet with parchment paper or nonstick foil.

2 Stir together flour, Italian seasoning, and ½ teaspoon salt in medium shallow dish. Stir together bread crumbs and oil in another shallow dish until evenly moistened.

3 Place egg whites and remaining ¼ teaspoon salt in medium bowl and with mixer on medium speed, beat until soft peaks form.

4 Working with few pieces at a time, place zucchini in flour mixture and toss to coat. Dip in egg white, shaking off excess. Dip in bread crumbs, pressing to adhere.

5 Arrange zucchini in single layer on prepared baking sheet. Spray with olive oil nonstick spray.

6 Bake, turning once, until lightly browned, about 12 minutes. Serve at once with lemon wedges.

(4) **SmartPoints value per serving** (about 10 pieces): 144 Cal, 5 g Total Fat, 1 g Sat Fat, 600 mg Sod, 18 g Total Carb, 3 g Sugar, 1 g Fib, 5 g Prot.

Eggplant, tomato, and feta stacks

serves 6   gluten free   vegetarian

1	**tablespoon lemon juice**
1	**tablespoon extra-virgin olive oil**
1	**tablespoon minced fresh oregano, plus additional leaves for garnish, optional**
1	**small garlic clove, minced**
¾	**teaspoon kosher salt**
1	**large eggplant, cut into 12 (½-inch) rounds**
¼	**teaspoon black pepper**
2	**large tomatoes, each cut into 6 slices**
¾	**cup crumbled feta**

1 Spray grill rack with nonstick spray and preheat grill to medium or prepare medium fire.

2 Stir together lemon juice, oil, 1 tablespoon oregano, garlic, and ¼ teaspoon salt in small bowl.

3 Lightly spray eggplant slices with olive oil nonstick spray; sprinkle with remaining ½ teaspoon salt and pepper.

4 Grill eggplant until tender, 4–5 minutes per side.

5 Brush top of each eggplant slice with lemon-juice mixture; top each with 1 slice tomato. Sprinkle each with 1 tablespoon feta. Cover and grill until tomatoes are slightly softened, about 1 minute.

6 Transfer to serving platter and garnish with oregano leaves, if using.

(3) **SmartPoints value per serving** (2 stacks): 106 Cal, 7 g Total Fat, 3 g Sat Fat, 456 mg Sod, 9 g Total Carb, 5 g Sugar, 3 g Fib, 4 g Prot.

Eat better
Grill some skinless boneless chicken breasts or salmon along with the veggies to make a delicious meal for zero additional Points.

Roasted Brussels sprouts with cranberries

serves 4   gluten free   vegetarian

1¼ **pounds fresh Brussels sprouts, trimmed and halved**

2   **teaspoons olive oil**

¾   **teaspoon salt**

¼   **teaspoon black pepper**

¼   **cup orange juice**

3   **tablespoons dried cranberries, coarsely chopped**

¼   **teaspoon grated orange zest**

2   **tablespoons walnuts, toasted and coarsely chopped**

1 Preheat oven to 450°F. Spray large rimmed baking sheet with nonstick spray.

2 Place Brussels sprouts in prepared pan; drizzle with oil and sprinkle with salt and pepper. Toss sprouts until coated evenly; spread to form even layer. Roast sprouts, stirring once, until tender and browned, 15–20 minutes.

3 Meanwhile, place orange juice in microwavable cup and microwave on High until hot, about 10 seconds. Add cranberries and let stand.

4 Transfer sprouts to medium bowl; stir in cranberry mixture and orange zest. Sprinkle with walnuts and serve.

(3) **SmartPoints value per serving** (¾ cup): 130 Cal, 5 g Total Fat, 1 g Sat Fat, 471 mg Sod, 19 g Total Carb, 8 g Sugar, 6 g Fib, 5 g Prot.

Lime yogurt with fruit and meringues, page 220

chapter 6

Creamy goodness: plain fat-free yogurt

Sweet and savory: 10 yogurt stir-ins and drizzle-ons for instant snacks

Packed with protein, loaded with good things like calcium and probiotics, and refreshingly creamy and tangy: There's a lot to love about yogurt. And choosing plain fat-free yogurt means you won't have to count it towards your SmartPoints Budget, making it a terrific snack choice.

What's the catch? Not everyone loves the flavor of yogurt by itself, and even devoted fans appreciate variety. So we rounded up ten easy add-ins that will help you enjoy it every day.

Greek yogurt has become the most popular for snacking, but all plain fat-free unsweetened dairy or soy yogurts are now zero Points, so select your favorite. Some of the ingredient suggestions below do have SmartPoints value, however, so be sure to measure and track those as needed.

Chopped veggies

Cucumber, sweet bell peppers, red onion, and more are excellent for adding a savory dimension to your yogurt. Try adding them with a little salt and pepper and a complementary spice like ground cumin or smoked paprika for depth of flavor.

Fresh fruit

Need we say more? From tropical mangoes and bananas to summer berries and apples to everything in between, fruit is the go-to partner to liven up your yogurt. Keep frozen unsweetened fruits on hand so you'll always have options.

Fresh herbs

Dill and chives are classic, but other leafy herbs like cilantro, parsley, basil, dill, and chervil are also excellent for bringing a delicious savory taste to yogurt. You'll get brighter flavor when you also add a touch of salt and pepper.

Granola

Turn to a topping of granola or another whole-grain cereal to make yogurt a satisfying mini-meal. Opt for brands with lower sugar and fat to get the most crunch from your SmartPoints.

Honey

It's the classic sweetener for yogurt, with a warm, rich flavor that blends deliciously with yogurt's natural tartness. Choose a flavorful wildflower honey and drizzle it on top for maximum impact.

Maple syrup

Sweet, aromatic pure maple syrup is ideal for transforming yogurt into a luscious snack or dessert. Add low-acid fruits like pears and bananas for a total comfort-food experience.

Nuts

You'll get a delicious dose of crunch from chopped nuts, and their natural oils make yogurt taste richer. You can also stir in nut butters for a silky treat. Don't forget coconut flakes: lusciously tropical and versatile enough for both sweet and savory snacking.

Olive oil

Really! A drizzle of fruity olive oil over yogurt and a generous sprinkle of coarse salt and black pepper turns Greek yogurt into a savory mouth-filling, Mediterranean-like spread or dip. Just go easy—1 teaspoon of oil (1 SmartPoints value) over ⅓ cup yogurt is plenty.

Unsweetened cocoa powder

Sometimes only chocolate will do the trick! Stir in cocoa powder and a sweetener and you'll find yogurt's acidity wonderfully tamed. A few drops of vanilla will round out the flavor. Eat it with a spoon for a pudding-like snack or use it as a dip with pretzels for a sweet-and-salty treat.

Vanilla extract

Aromatic pure vanilla: It softens yogurt's distinctive tang and tricks our taste buds into thinking we're eating something sweeter than it really is. Give almond and chocolate extracts a try for variety.

Give plain yogurt a flavor upgrade with nuts, fresh or dried fruits, honey, or fresh herbs.

Fall fruit and yogurt breakfast bowls

serves 2   gluten free   no cook   vegetarian   under 20 minutes

This honey-sweetened yogurt is the perfect base for topping with any mixture of fresh fruit you have on hand. Add some crunch by sprinkling each serving with up to ½ tablespoon toasted sliced almonds for no additional SmartPoints value.

1½ **cups plain fat-free Greek yogurt**

1½ **teaspoons honey**

1   **cup grapes, halved**

4   **fresh figs, quartered**

¼   **cup pomegranate arils**

1 Whisk together yogurt and honey in medium bowl.

2 Divide yogurt mixture evenly between 2 bowls. Top with grapes and figs and sprinkle with pomegranate arils.

1 **SmartPoints value per serving** (¾ cup yogurt mixture, ¾ cup fruit, and 2 tablespoons pomegranate arils): 260 Cal, 2 g Total Fat, 0 g Sat Fat, 66 mg Sod, 47 g Total Carb, 41 g Sugar, 4 g Fib, 20 g Prot.

Blueberry-nectarine spoon fruit with yogurt

serves 6   **gluten free**   **vegetarian**

To make this dessert ahead of time, prepare the recipe through step 1. Store the fruit mixture in an airtight container in the refrigerator for up to four days. Assemble just before serving.

1   pint fresh blueberries

2   nectarines, pitted and sliced

¼   cup unsweetened apple juice

1   tablespoon maple syrup

1   teaspoon vanilla extract

3   cups plain fat-free Greek yogurt

3   tablespoons walnuts, toasted and chopped

1 Combine blueberries, nectarines, apple juice, and maple syrup in medium saucepan and bring to boil. Reduce heat and simmer until nectarines are softened, about 5 minutes. Remove from heat and stir in vanilla. Transfer to large shallow dish and cool slightly.

2 Spoon ½ cup fruit mixture into each of 6 bowls; top each with ½ cup yogurt and sprinkle evenly with walnuts.

2 **SmartPoints value per serving** (1 bowl): 155 Cal, 3 g Total Fat, 0 g Sat Fat, 42 mg Sod, 20 g Total Carb, 16 g Sugar, 2 g Fib, 13 g Prot.

Strawberry yogurt and fruit parfaits

serves 4   gluten free   no cook   vegetarian   under 20 minutes

4   cups plain fat-free Greek yogurt

¼   cup low-sugar strawberry preserves

4   navel oranges

2   cups strawberries, hulled and sliced

2   bananas, thinly sliced

1   teaspoon grated peeled fresh ginger

4   tablespoons sliced almonds, toasted

1 Whisk together yogurt and preserves in medium bowl until blended. Set aside.

2 With small knife, cut away peel and white pith from oranges. Working over another medium bowl, cut between membranes to release segments. Add strawberries, bananas, and ginger to bowl and stir to combine.

3 Layer fruit mixture and yogurt mixture evenly into 4 parfait glasses. Sprinkle parfaits evenly with almonds.

2 **SmartPoints value per serving** (1 parfait): 329 Cal, 4 g Total Fat, 1 g Sat Fat, 82 mg Sod, 50 g Total Carb, 35 g Sugar, 7 g Fib, 27 g Prot.

Strawberry yogurt
and fruit parfaits

Greek yogurt with cherry compote

Greek yogurt with cherry compote

serves 4   **gluten free**   **vegetarian**

When buying cherries for this recipe, be sure to choose sweet cherries instead of sour cherries. Sweet cherries are naturally sweet enough to eat on their own, but sour cherries will make your mouth pucker unless they are prepared with a generous amount of sugar.

1⅓ **cups fresh sweet cherries, pitted and halved, or unsweetened frozen pitted cherries, halved**

½ **cup orange juice**

2 **teaspoons honey**

1 **(3-inch) cinnamon stick**

¼ **teaspoon salt**

2 **cups plain fat-free Greek yogurt**

2 **tablespoons finely chopped toasted pistachios**

1 To make compote, combine cherries, orange juice, honey, cinnamon stick, and salt in small saucepan and bring to boil over medium heat. Reduce heat to medium-low and simmer, stirring occasionally, until cherries soften and liquid begins to thicken slightly, about 12 minutes.

2 Transfer to medium bowl; remove and discard cinnamon stick. Set bowl inside large bowl or sink filled with ice water and cool, stirring occasionally. (Or, refrigerate, covered, until chilled, about 4 hours. The sauce may be made up to 4 days ahead and stored in covered container in refrigerator.)

3 To serve, divide yogurt evenly among 4 bowls. Top evenly with compote and sprinkle evenly with pistachios.

2 SmartPoints value per serving (1 bowl): 139 Cal, 2 g Total Fat, 0 g Sat Fat, 187 mg Sod, 18 g Total Carb, 14 g Sugar, 2 g Fib, 13 g Prot.

Lime yogurt with fruit and meringues

serves 4   gluten free   no cook   vegetarian   under 20 minutes

Keep this adaptable recipe in your regular rotation and vary it using orange, tangerine, clementine, or lemon zest instead of the lime zest. And the fruit topping? Whatever is fresh and available will be delicious! Crumbling a meringue over each serving lends a touch of sweetness and crunch to every bite.

1   cup plain fat-free Greek yogurt

1   tablespoon sugar

¾   teaspoon grated lime zest

Pinch salt

1   large mango, peeled, pitted, and chopped

1   (6-ounce) package fresh raspberries

1   cup fresh blueberries

4   (2-inch) purchased meringues

1 Stir together yogurt, sugar, lime zest, and salt in small bowl.

2 Gently toss together mango, raspberries, and blueberries in medium bowl.

3 Divide yogurt mixture evenly among 4 shallow bowls; top evenly with mango mixture. Crumble 1 meringue over each bowl and serve at once.

2 **SmartPoints value per serving** (1 dessert): 161 Cal, 1 g Total Fat, 0 g Sat Fat, 96 mg Sod, 34 g Total Carb, 27 g Sugar, 5 g Fib, 7 g Prot.

Lime yogurt with fruit and meringues

Nectarines and yogurt with bourbon sauce

serves 4   gluten free   vegetarian

½ cup unsweetened tropical fruit juice blend

3 tablespoons packed light brown sugar

1½ teaspoons cornstarch

1 tablespoon bourbon

1 teaspoon unsalted butter

¼ teaspoon vanilla extract

4 nectarines, halved and pitted

1⅓ cups plain fat-free Greek yogurt

1 To make sauce, stir together juice, brown sugar, and cornstarch in small saucepan until smooth. Set over medium heat and cook, stirring occasionally, until mixture comes to boil and thickens, about 2 minutes. Remove from heat and stir in bourbon, butter, and vanilla. Pour into a shallow dish to cool slightly. Set aside.

2 Spray large ridged grill pan with nonstick spray and set over medium heat. Spray nectarines lightly with nonstick spray. Place cut side down in grill pan and grill until slightly softened, about 2 minutes on each side.

3 Divide nectarines evenly among 4 shallow bowls; top evenly with yogurt and sauce.

4 **SmartPoints value per serving** (2 nectarine halves, ⅓ cup yogurt, and 2 tablespoons sauce): 182 Cal, 2 g Total Fat, 1 g Sat Fat, 39 mg Sod, 32 g Total Carb, 27 g Sugar, 2 g Fib, 9 g Prot.

Greek yogurt with warm blueberry sauce

serves 6   **gluten free**   **vegetarian**

2   cups fresh blueberries
2   tablespoons sugar
2   tablespoons water
½   teaspoon grated lemon zest
½   teaspoon fresh lemon juice
Pinch salt
3   cups plain fat-free Greek yogurt

1 Combine blueberries, sugar, and water in medium saucepan; set over medium-high heat and bring to boil. Reduce heat and simmer, stirring occasionally, until most blueberries burst and sauce is slightly thickened, 5–7 minutes.

2 Transfer sauce to medium bowl; stir in lemon zest and juice and salt. Let cool slightly. (Sauce can be made up to 4 days ahead and stored in covered container in refrigerator.)

3 Spoon yogurt evenly into bowls; top with sauce and swirl into yogurt.

(1) **SmartPoints value per serving** (½ cup yogurt and about ¼ cup sauce): 111 Cal, 1 g Total Fat, 0 g Sat Fat, 90 mg Sod, 15 g Total Carb, 13 g Sugar, 1 g Fib, 12 g Prot.

Eat better
Indulge by topping this low SmartPoints value dessert with 1 tablespoon toasted sliced almonds for 1 additional SmartPoints value.

Yogurt with rhubarb-raspberry sauce

serves 12   **gluten free**   **vegetarian**

This simple sauce is a delicious introduction to rhubarb's tart, earthy flavor. No matter how gently you cook it, rhubarb falls apart as soon as it becomes tender, so you won't see the pretty red slices after it is cooked.

½ **cup water**

¼ **cup granulated sugar**

¼ **cup packed light brown sugar**

1 **pound fresh rhubarb, trimmed and thinly sliced, or 1 (10-ounce) box frozen sliced rhubarb, thawed**

1 **(6-ounce) container fresh raspberries**

6 **cups plain fat-free Greek yogurt**

6 **tablespoons sliced almonds, toasted**

1 Combine water, granulated sugar, and brown sugar in medium saucepan and set over medium-high heat. Cook, stirring frequently, until sugars dissolve, about 2 minutes.

2 Add rhubarb and cook, stirring often, until just tender, 5–7 minutes. Add raspberries and cook, stirring often, until berries just begin to fall apart, about 3 minutes. Transfer to medium bowl. Set bowl inside large bowl or sink filled with ice water and cool, stirring occasionally. (Or, refrigerate, covered, until chilled, about 4 hours. The sauce may be made up to 4 days ahead and stored in covered container in refrigerator.)

3 For each serving, spoon ½ cup yogurt into small bowl. Top with 2 tablespoons sauce and ½ tablespoon almonds.

3 **SmartPoints value per serving** (1 dessert): 129 Cal, 2 g Total Fat, 0 g Sat Fat, 44 mg Sod, 16 g Total Carb, 13 g Sugar, 2 g Fib, 13 g Prot.

Walnut dip

serves 8 as an appetizer or snack   **gluten free**   **no cook**   **vegetarian**   **under 20 minutes**

This versatile dip goes well with fresh raw veggies, but it's also great served as a sauce for shrimp, fish, or chicken. If you have time, toast the walnuts in a 350°F oven for 6 to 8 minutes until fragrant, before making the recipe.

1½ **cups plain fat-free Greek yogurt**
⅓   **cup walnuts, finely chopped**
3   **tablespoons lemon juice**
2   **garlic cloves, minced**
1½ **tablespoons chopped fresh dill**
1   **tablespoon extra-virgin olive oil**
¾   **teaspoon salt**
1   **teaspoon paprika**

Stir together all ingredients except paprika in medium bowl. Sprinkle with paprika just before serving.

2 **SmartPoints value per serving** (¼ cup): 75 Cal, 5 g Total Fat, 1 g Sat Fat, 234 mg Sod, 3 g Total Carb, 2 g Sugar, 0 g Fib, 5 g Prot.

Cucumber-yogurt dip with pita chips

Cucumber-yogurt dip with pita chips

serves 4 as an appetizer or snack   **vegetarian**

If you don't care for the flavor of dill, use mint, cilantro, or basil in this recipe. While you're at it, make a double batch and use it for dipping fresh vegetables or as a sauce for salmon or shrimp. It can be refrigerated for up to four days.

2	**(6-inch) whole wheat pita breads**
1	**cup diced English (seedless) cucumber**
1	**cup plain fat-free Greek yogurt**
2	**tablespoons chopped fresh dill, plus additional for garnish**
1	**small garlic clove, minced**
1	**teaspoon lemon juice**
1	**teaspoon ground cumin**
½	**teaspoon salt**
⅛	**teaspoon cayenne**

1 Preheat oven to 400°F.

2 To make chips, lightly coat both sides of each pita with olive oil nonstick spray. Cut each pita into 8 wedges; arrange wedges in single layer on large baking sheet. Bake until crisp and lightly toasted, 6–7 minutes. Transfer to rack to cool.

3 Meanwhile, to make dip, stir together remaining ingredients in medium bowl. Sprinkle with additional dill. Serve dip with pita chips.

1 **SmartPoints value per serving** (generous ¼ cup dip with 4 pita triangles): 78 Cal, 1 g Total Fat, 0 g Sat Fat, 387 mg Sod, 11 g Total Carb, 2 g Sugar, 1 g Fib, 7 g Prot.

Green goddess dip

Green goddess dip

serves 4 as an appetizer or snack   **gluten free**   **no cook**   **vegetarian**   **under 20 minutes**

¾ cup plain fat-free Greek yogurt

¼ cup chopped fresh chives, plus additional for garnish

2 tablespoons chopped fresh dill

1 scallion, sliced

1 tablespoon chopped fresh mint

1 tablespoon extra-virgin olive oil

½ teaspoon salt

¼ teaspoon cracked black pepper, plus additional for garnish

Puree all ingredients in blender or food processor. Spoon into serving bowl; sprinkle with additional chives and cracked black pepper. Serve with vegetable crudités or use as a salad dressing.

1 **SmartPoints value per serving** (3 tablespoons): 58 Cal, 4 g Total Fat, 1 g Sat Fat, 307 mg Sod, 2 g Total Carb, 1 g Sugar, 0 g Fib, 5 g Prot.

Let's do this together

Up for a challenge? Try member Sheri Friedman's time-saving grocery shopping strategy: "Sometimes I challenge myself to shop in a certain time frame. I imagine I'm on one of those game shows and I have to get everything I need by a certain time. It keeps me from getting distracted!"

Strawberry-mascarpone-topped cookies, page 240

chapter 7
Naturally sweet: fruits

Make fruit a healthy habit

When foods as delicious as succulent strawberries, crisp apples, and vibrant oranges are 0 SmartPoints value, who needs anything else for a snack or dessert? Fruits are great sources of fiber, vitamins, minerals, and antioxidants and their natural sweetness makes them a welcome treat when you're craving something sweet. These tips will help you choose, store, and enjoy more fresh fruits every day.

Buying

Use common sense when shopping for fruit. Look for fruits with vibrant colors and tight skins without wrinkles or signs of decay. Buy fruits locally in season as often as you can for better flavor and to support your local farmers.

To taste best, fruit has to be ripe, so plan ahead. Apricots, bananas, cantaloupe, honeydew, kiwifruit, mangos, nectarines, peaches, pears, pineapples, and plums will ripen after picking, so leave these on the kitchen counter until they reach peak ripeness and become fragrant.

Other fruits, including apples, berries, citrus, and grapes, will not ripen after picking, so they are ready to eat as soon as you buy them.

Don't forget frozen and canned fruits. Choose unsweetened frozen fruits to make desserts and smoothies. Canned fruits that are unsweetened, artificially sweetened, or packed in water are also zero Points foods and make convenient snacks.

Storing

What you see is what you eat, and if there's a luscious bowl of fresh fruit on your kitchen counter at all times, you're more likely to snack on an orange instead of rummaging through the snack drawer for a higher SmartPoints value nibble.

Highly perishable berries should always be refrigerated, but apart from them, always keep some fruit out where you'll see it. If it's more appealing, cut up a combination of fruits and store them in a clear container in the front of the refrigerator. These ready-to-eat treats will be the first snack or dessert option you see when you open the door.

Enjoying

Top your breakfast oatmeal, cereal, or yogurt with fruit to make the first meal of the day a little sweeter.

Fruit is a nutritous and handy zero Points snack for any time of day. Always carry a piece of fresh fruit with you to work or when running errands. These natural go-to foods will prevent you from getting too hungry before your next meal.

Try grilling, broiling, or roasting fresh fruit. All of these methods help bring out the sweetness of almost any fruit. Turn cooked fruit into a tasty dessert by topping with a spoonful of plain fat-free Greek yogurt and a sprinkle of toasted nuts.

Snack smart. All fresh fruits are zero Points, so keep a variety on hand for eating at home and on the go.

Try out-of-the-ordinary fruits. Add some sweet lychees to a fruit salad or snack on dragon fruit (it tastes like a cross between pear and kiwifruit).

Mango-avocado salsa

serves 12   gluten free   no cook   vegetarian   under 20 minutes

For an appetizer or a snack, serve this salsa with baked tortilla chips (12 baked low-fat tortilla chips have 3 SmartPoints value), or zero Points Belgian endive leaves. It's also delicious with any type of grilled or broiled fish or ordinary chicken breast.

1	**large Hass avocado, peeled, pitted, and diced**
1	**large mango, peeled, pitted, and diced**
1	**large tomato, chopped**
2	**tablespoons diced red onion**
2	**tablespoons lime juice**
2	**tablespoons chopped fresh cilantro**
⅛	**teaspoon salt**

Place all ingredients in medium bowl and toss gently.

1 **SmartPoints value per serving** (¼ cup): 44 Cal, 2 g Total Fat, 0 g Sat Fat, 26 mg Sod, 7 g Total Carb, 5 g Sugar, 2 g Fib, 1 g Prot.

Mango-avocado salsa

Chocolate-dipped baby bananas

Chocolate-dipped baby bananas

serves 12   gluten free   vegetarian

This fun dessert is perfect to serve at a casual party. Kids and adults can't resist the banana and chocolate combination. If you can't find baby bananas, use four regular bananas and cut each one crosswise into thirds.

12 **baby bananas, peeled**

3 **ounces semisweet chocolate, chopped**

¾ **teaspoon unsalted butter**

2 **tablespoons shredded unsweetened coconut, toasted**

1 Line large baking sheet with wax paper. Insert wooden craft stick or short wooden skewer in one end of each banana.

2 Combine chocolate and butter in medium microwavable bowl. Microwave on High, 1 minute. Stir until smooth.

3 Working with 1 banana at a time, spoon chocolate over bananas to cover. Sprinkle bananas with coconut and place on baking sheet. Refrigerate until chocolate sets, about 15 minutes.

2 **SmartPoints value per serving** (1 baby banana): 77 Cal, 3 g Total Fat, 2 g Sat Fat, 1 mg Sod,14 g Total Carb, 9 g Sugar, 2 g Fib, 1 g Prot.

Melon and prosciutto with fennel

serves 2   gluten free   no cook   under 20 minutes

¼ **cantaloupe, peeled, seeded, and cut into 6 wedges**

¼ **teaspoon fennel seeds, crushed, or to taste**

¼ **teaspoon cracked black pepper**

2 **slices lean prosciutto, halved crosswise**

Lemon wedges

Place 3 melon wedges on each of 2 small plates; sprinkle evenly with fennel and pepper. Top each serving with 2 strips prosciutto.Serve with lemon wedges.

(1) **SmartPoints value per serving** (1 plate): 61 Cal, 2 g Total Fat, 1 g Sat Fat, 266 mg Sod, 8 g Total Carb, 6 g Sugar, 1 g Fib, 5 g Prot.

Strawberries with ginger-lemon sugar

serves 4   gluten free   no cook   vegetarian   under 20 minutes

2   tablespoons sugar

1   teaspoon finely chopped crystallized ginger

½   teaspoon grated lemon zest

1   (1-pound) container strawberries, hulled and quartered

1 Process sugar, ginger, and lemon zest in coffee or spice grinder until finely ground.

2 Place strawberries in medium bowl; sprinkle with sugar mixture and toss to coat. Let stand until berries begin to release their juices, about 5 minutes. Serve at room temperature.

(2) **SmartPoints value per serving** (¾ cup): 64 Cal, 0 g Total Fat, 0 g Sat Fat, 1 mg Sod, 16 g Total Carb, 13 g Total Sugar, 2 g Fib, 1 g Prot.

Eat better

Serve the strawberries over plain fat-free Greek yogurt for no additional SmartPoints.

Strawberry-mascarpone-topped cookies

serves 6   no cook   vegetarian   under 20 minutes

We used Bahlsen brand Afrika dark chocolate-covered wafers for this recipe. If you can't find those, try using the more commonly available Nabisco Famous Chocolate Wafers. Either way, the chocolate, cheese, and fruit combination is irresistible. Arrange them on a pretty tray or platter for an easy, yet elegant finish to any meal.

1	**cup strawberries, hulled and thinly sliced**
½	**teaspoon sugar**
½	**teaspoon lemon juice**
¼	**cup mascarpone**
12	**chocolate-covered wafer cookies**
1	**tablespoon chopped fresh mint**

1 Toss together strawberries, sugar, and lemon juice in small bowl.

2 Spread 1 teaspoon mascarpone onto each cookie; top evenly with strawberry mixture. Sprinkle cookies evenly with mint.

5 **SmartPoints value per serving** (2 topped cookies): 96 Cal, 7 g Total Fat, 5 g Sat Fat, 6 mg Sod, 7 g Total Carb, 5 g Sugar, 1 g Fib, 1 g Prot.

Strawberry-mascarpone-topped cookies

**Melon with
lime syrup**

Melon with lime syrup

serves 4   gluten free   vegetarian

2   tablespoons sugar

½   teaspoon grated lime zest

1   tablespoon lime juice

1   tablespoon cold water

½   large cantaloupe, seeded, peeled, and cut into 1-inch cubes

1   cup (1-inch) cubes seedless watermelon

1   (6-ounce) container fresh raspberries

2   tablespoons finely chopped crystallized ginger

1 Stir together sugar, lime zest and juice, and water in cup. Let stand 5 minutes, stirring occasionally, until sugar dissolves.

2 Divide cantaloupe, watermelon, and raspberries among 4 dessert dishes. Drizzle lime syrup evenly over each serving and sprinkle evenly with ginger.

2 **SmartPoints value per serving** (1 dessert): 98 Cal, 1 g Total Fat, 0 g Sat Fat, 18 mg Sod, 24 g Total Carb, 20 g Sugar, 4 g Fib, 1 g Prot.

Eat better

If you love the taste of ginger, topping fresh fruits or plain fat-free Greek yogurt with chopped crystallized ginger is a delicious way to add a touch of sweetness and bold flavor. Enjoy up to 2 teaspoons of chopped crystallized ginger for no additional SmartPoints.

Fruit kebabs with creamy raspberry sauce

serves 6   **gluten free**   **no cook**   **vegetarian**

- **2** cups thawed frozen unsweetened raspberries
- **¼** cup plain fat-free Greek yogurt
- **2** tablespoons honey
- **¼** cantaloupe, peeled, seeded, and cut into large chunks
- **¼** honeydew melon, peeled, seeded, and cut into large chunks
- **1** kiwi, peeled and cut into chunks
- **12** strawberries, hulled
- **1** banana, cut into 1-inch chunks
- **¾** cup large red seedless grapes

1 To make sauce, pulse raspberries in food processor until pureed. Strain puree through sieve set over bowl; discard seeds. Stir yogurt and honey into puree.

2 To make kebabs, thread fruits evenly on 6 (10-inch) wooden skewers. (Fruit can be skewered 1–2 hours ahead, covered, and refrigerated.) Serve with sauce.

① **SmartPoints value per serving** (1 skewer and 2½ tablespoons sauce): 123 Cal, 1 g Total Fat, 0 g Sat Fat, 19 mg Sod, 30 g Total Carb, 22 g Sugar, 5 g Fib, 3 g Prot.

Let's do this together

Member Sarah Ashley Pratt is a huge fan of saving time by buying precut fruit. "It's a bit more expensive, but I like buying the huge fruit salad bowls at my supermarket," she says. This creamy raspberry sauce would make the perfect accompaniment to fresh fruit of any kind.

Apricots with buttery gingersnap crumbs

serves 4   no cook   vegetarian   under 20 minutes

3   gingersnap cookies, crushed

4   teaspoons pistachios, coarsely chopped

1   teaspoon butter, melted

4   apricots, halved and pitted

4   tablespoons plain fat-free Greek yogurt

1 Combine gingersnaps, pistachios, and butter in small bowl until evenly moistened.

2 Divide apricots cut side up between 4 small plates. Sprinkle evenly with crumb mixture. Top evenly with yogurt.

2   **SmartPoints value per serving** (2 apricot halves, 1 tablespoon crumb mixture, and 1 tablespoon yogurt): 69 Cal, 3 g Total Fat, 1 g Sat Fat, 32 mg Sod, 9 g Total Carb, 5 g Sugar, 1 g Fib, 3 g Prot.

Strawberry yogurt with sugared pumpkin seeds

serves 4   gluten free   vegetarian

If keeping frozen yogurt or ice cream on hand is too much of a temptation, this almost-instant dessert is a refreshing option. Top each serving with a handful of fresh strawberries for a pretty garnish.

3   **tablespoons raw shelled pumpkin seeds**

1½   **teaspoons granulated sugar**

⅛   **teaspoon salt**

2   **tablespoons superfine sugar**

1   **(14-ounce) bag frozen unsweetened sliced strawberries**

⅓   **cup plain fat-free yogurt**

2   **tablespoons lime juice**

1   **tablespoon tequila (optional)**

1 Spray small baking sheet with nonstick spray.

2 Place pumpkin seeds in small nonstick skillet. Set over medium heat and cook, stirring frequently, until seeds begin to pop, about 4 minutes. Sprinkle pumpkin seeds with granulated sugar and cook, stirring constantly, until sugar melts and coats seeds, about 1 minute. Spread seeds on baking sheet. Sprinkle with salt and set aside to cool.

3 Place superfine sugar in food processor; process until very finely ground, 1 minute. Add strawberries and pulse until finely chopped (let thaw slightly to soften, if needed). Add yogurt, lime juice, and tequila, if using, and process until smooth. Divide evenly among 4 bowls, sprinkle evenly with pumpkin seeds, and serve at once.

3   **SmartPoints value per serving** (1 dessert): 114 Cal, 3 g Total Fat, 1 g Sat Fat, 90 mg Sod, 19 g Total Carb, 14 g Sugar, 3 g Fib, 3 g Prot.

Strawberry yogurt with sugared pumpkin seeds

**Blueberries with ricotta
and balsamic glaze**

Blueberries with ricotta and balsamic glaze

serves 4   gluten free   no cook   vegetarian   under 20 minutes

Whipping the ricotta takes away its grainy texture and makes it light, creamy, and fluffy. Use it as a topping for any kind of fruit to make a quick, yet distinctive dessert.

1   cup fat-free ricotta
2   teaspoons grated orange zest
2   pints fresh blueberries
2   teaspoons balsamic glaze

1   Puree ricotta in mini- or regular food processor. Scrape cheese into small bowl and stir in orange zest.

2   Divide blueberries evenly among 4 dessert dishes; top evenly with ricotta mixture and drizzle evenly with balsamic glaze.

2 **SmartPoints value per serving** (1 dessert): 144 Cal, 1 g Total Fat, 0 g Sat Fat, 124 mg Sod, 27 g Total Carb, 19 g Sugar, 4 g Fib, 10 g Prot.

Sugar-roasted plums with rosemary

serves 4   gluten free   vegetarian

4 red or black plums, halved and pitted

2 tablespoons balsamic vinegar

3 tablespoons brown sugar

1 tablespoon minced fresh rosemary

1 Preheat oven to 400°F. Spray 9-inch square baking dish with nonstick spray.

2 Arrange plums cut side up in baking dish. Drizzle with vinegar; sprinkle with brown sugar and rosemary. Roast until juices are bubbling and plums are tender, about 20 minutes.

2 **SmartPoints value per serving** (2 plum halves): 64 Cal, 0 g Total Fat, 0 g Sat Fat, 4 mg Sod, 16 g Total Carb, 14 g Sugar, 1 g Fib, 1 g Prot.

Eat better

For a creamy finish, serve the plums over zero Points plain fat-free Greek yogurt. You can try the simple roasting technique used in this recipe with nectarines or peaches, too.

Fresh fruit compote with orange liqueur

serves 6   gluten free   vegetarian

If you don't have orange liqueur, you can substitute any fruit-flavored liqueur in this recipe. Try pomegranate, lemon, or raspberry, or leave it out and the compote will still be a fantastic dessert.

3   **large ruby grapefruits**

3   **cups strawberries, hulled and halved**

1   **tablespoon sugar**

Pinch salt

2   **tablespoons orange liqueur**

2   **teaspoons chopped fresh tarragon**

1   With sharp knife, peel 2 grapefruits, removing all white pith. Working over sieve set over bowl, cut between the membranes to release segments. Squeeze juice from membranes into sieve over small bowl, then discard membranes. Transfer grapefruit segments to large bowl; add strawberries.

2   Squeeze juice from remaining grapefruit into small bowl to get ¾ cup juice (reserve any remaining juice for another use). Combine juice, sugar, and salt in medium nonreactive skillet and bring to boil over medium-high heat. Cook until reduced to ⅓ cup, about 4 minutes. Transfer to small shallow heatproof bowl to cool slightly.

3   Add grapefruit syrup and liqueur to grapefruit and strawberries and stir gently to combine. Sprinkle with tarragon just before serving.

1   **SmartPoints value per serving** (½ cup): 101 Cal, 0 g Total Fat, 0 g Sat Fat, 49 mg Sod, 24 g Total Carb, 20 g Sugar, 3 g Fib, 2 g Prot.

Spice-roasted pears

Spice-roasted pears

serves 4   gluten free   vegetarian

To prep the pears, use a vegetable peeler to peel them, then slice them in half lengthwise. Use a teaspoon or melon baller to carefully scoop out the cores, the line that runs up to the stem, and the bud at the bottom of each pear.

4	**ripe Bartlett or Comice pears, peeled, halved lengthwise, and cored**
1	**tablespoon lemon juice**
¾	**teaspoon cinnamon**
⅛	**teaspoon ground allspice**
1	**tablespoon butter, melted**
¼	**cup plain fat-free Greek yogurt**

1 Preheat oven to 450°F. Line large baking sheet with nonstick foil.

2 Combine pears, lemon juice, cinnamon, and allspice in medium bowl; toss well.

3 With sharp knife, cut each pear half lengthwise almost through to the base into ¼-inch-thick slices, keeping the base intact. Carefully transfer the sliced pear halves to the baking sheet with a spatula. Gently press down on each half to fan the slices open slightly. Drizzle with butter. Bake until the pears are tender, 15–20 minutes.

4 Top evenly with yogurt and serve at once.

1 **SmartPoints value per serving** (2 pear halves and 1 tablespoon yogurt): 148 Cal, 3 g Total Fat, 2 g Sat Fat, 30 mg Sod, 28 g Total Carb, 18 g Sugar, 6 g Fib, 2 g Prot.

Turkey pita
pizzas, page 56

Recipes by SmartPoints value

0 SmartPoints value
Chicken and kale salad with miso dressing, 15
Minted zucchini and cherry tomatoes, 202
Stir-fried ginger spinach, 194

1 SmartPoints value
Arctic char with watercress salad, 81
Black bean–tomatillo dip, 125
Cabbage salad with lime-Sriracha dressing, 191
Carrot, snow pea, and bean stir-fry, 135
Chicken with strawberry-balsamic salsa, 4
Corn, tomato, and shrimp sauté, 95
Corn, zucchini, and tomatoes with cilantro, 196
Cucumber, honeydew, and pepitas salad, 183
Cucumber-yogurt dip with pita chips, 227
Fall fruit and yogurt breakfast bowls, 214
Five-spice turkey with mushrooms, 52
Fresh fruit compote with orange liqueur, 251
Fresh pea soup with mint, 174
Fruit kebabs with creamy raspberry sauce, 244
Greek yogurt with warm blueberry sauce, 223
Green bean and tomato sauté, 199
Green goddess dip, 229
Grilled bell peppers with olive vinaigrette, 181
Grilled chicken with indian spices, 6
Grilled salmon with ginger-scallion sauce, 66
Grilled salmon with pea and corn salad, 69
Lemon-basil chicken-and-vegetable kebabs, 22
Lemon-curry chickpea and celery salad, 139
Mango-avocado salsa, 234
Melon and prosciutto with fennel, 238
Microwave broccoli with spicy garlic oil, 190
Moroccan vegetable stew, 134
Paprika chicken with orange-olive relish, 9

Parmesan-basil broiled tomatoes, 200
Quick bbq chicken breasts, 12
Quick gazpacho, 172
Roasted asparagus and red bell pepper with dill, 193
Roasted bell peppers and radicchio, 195
Shrimp, bell pepper, and thyme frittata, 154
Smoky turkey gumbo, 37
Spiced edamame and green bean stew, 115
Spice-roasted pears, 255
Tandoori roasted salmon with vegetables, 72
Tuna with caramelized onions and fennel, 74
Turkey tacos in lettuce wraps, 51

2 SmartPoints value
Adzuki-edamame salad with miso dressing, 119
Apricots with buttery gingersnap crumbs, 245
Blueberries with ricotta and balsamic glaze, 249
Blueberry-nectarine spoon fruit with yogurt, 215
Chicken and broccoli slaw with cashews, 25
Chicken salad with cucumber-yogurt sauce, 11
Chicken satay with red curry–peanut sauce, 20
Chocolate-dipped baby bananas, 237
Cornmeal spice–crusted tilapia, 84
Five-spice tofu and vegetable stir-fry, 113
Greek salad with feta and artichokes, 186
Greek yogurt with cherry compote, 219
Green bean salad with ricotta salata, 185
Green salad with carrot vinaigrette, 184
Lentil, strawberry, and watercress salad, 141
Lime yogurt with fruit and meringues, 220
Melon with lime syrup, 243
Salmon and Kalamata olive sandwiches, 83
Sautéed tilapia with almonds and cherries, 75
Shrimp and cherry tomatoes with feta, 94

**Black bean–tomatillo
dip, page 125**

Arctic char with
watercress salad,
page 81

Index

**Gingery turkey
noodle soup, page 38**

Measurement equivalents

If you are converting the recipes in this book to metric measurements, use the following chart as a guide.

Teaspoons	Tablespoons	Cups	Fluid Ounces	Volume	
3 teaspoons	1 tablespoon		½ fluid ounce	¼ teaspoon	1 milliliter
6 teaspoons	2 tablespoons	⅛ cup	1 fluid ounce	½ teaspoon	2 milliliters
8 teaspoons	2 tablespoons plus 2 teaspoons	⅙ cup		1 teaspoon	5 milliliters
12 teaspoons	4 tablespoons	¼ cup	2 fluid ounces	1 tablespoon	15 milliliters
15 teaspoons	5 tablespoons	⅓ cup minus 1 teaspoon		2 tablespoons	30 milliliters
16 teaspoons	5 tablespoons plus 1 teaspoon	⅓ cup		3 tablespoons	45 milliliters
18 teaspoons	6 tablespoons	¼ cup plus 2 tablespoons	3 fluid ounces	¼ cup	60 milliliters
24 teaspoons	8 tablespoons	½ cup	4 fluid ounces	⅓ cup	80 milliliters
30 teaspoons	10 tablespoons	½ cup plus 2 tablespoons	5 fluid ounces	½ cup	120 milliliters
32 teaspoons	10 tablespoons plus 2 teaspoons	⅔ cup		⅔ cup	160 milliliters
36 teaspoons	12 tablespoons	¾ cup	6 fluid ounces	¾ cup	175 milliliters
42 teaspoons	14 tablespoons	1 cup minus 2 tablespoons	7 fluid ounces	1 cup	240 milliliters
45 teaspoons	15 tablespoons	1 cup minus 1 tablespoon		1 quart	950 milliliters
48 teaspoons	16 tablespoons	1 cup	8 fluid ounces		

Length

1 inch	25 millimeters
1 inch	2.5 centimeters

Oven Temperature

250°F	120°C	400°F	200°C
275°F	140°C	425°F	220°C
300°F	150°C	450°F	230°C
325°F	160°C	475°F	250°C
350°F	180°C	500°F	260°C
375°F	190°C	525°F	270°C

Weight

1 ounce	30 grams
¼ pound	120 grams
½ pound	240 grams
¾ pound	340 grams
1 pound	480 grams

Note: Measurement of less than ⅛ teaspoon is considered a dash or a pinch. Metric measurements are approximate.